IS THE FUTURE MY RESPONSIBILITY?

OUR SOCIETY IN THE NEW MILLENNIUM

EDITED BY
HARRY BOHAN
AND GERARD KENNEDY

VERITAS

ESB has always been highly regarded for its long-term management capabilities. While we are driven by, and react to, the needs of our customers, we are also conscious that we are a company whose policies, and the activities which flow from these, affect everyone living and working in Ireland, not just our 1.5m customers.

It is our view that we must ensure we understand the changing interface between and within communities in which we all work and live. Without such an understanding we will face difficulties in serving our customers and consumers. It is a measure of this concern that we have continued our sponsorship of this annual Conference 'Our Society in the New Millennium'.

BARNEY WHELAN
ESB, Public Relations Manager
Conference Sponsor

First published 2002 by
Veritas Publications
7/8 Lower Abbey Street
Dublin 1
Ireland

Email publications@veritas.ie
Website www.veritas.ie

ISBN 1 85390 605 0

A catalogue record for this book is available from the British Library.

Cover design by Avid Design
Printed in the Republic of Ireland by Betaprint Ltd, Dublin

CONTENTS

FOREWORD

Irish society is now an opening and questioning one – certainly more open and more questioning than seemed possible twenty-five years ago. Exposure to the global culture is intensive, progress towards European integration is of historic proportions. The changes have major implications for the way people live their lives. Relationships, critical to meaning in life, will be more a matter of choice than a legacy into which you are born.

The twentieth century was the age of the organisation person. People were educated and shaped for a world of institutions. These in turn wrote the script that shaped our lives. One thing that has been learned in the latter half of the twentieth century is that centrally planned systems do not meet people's needs.

New styles of social institutions are evolving. The relationship between people and institutions needs to be redefined and new ways of responding found. Individual freedom is valued but freedom must be balanced with responsibility.

The papers contained in this publication will hopefully give some pointers as to what direction we need to take. Just as the twentieth century emphasised material values this new century will focus on the life of the spirit. So we are challenged to discover a spirituality that helps people to feel a sense of worth and to take responsibility for their future. It will need to be a strong spirituality, a spirituality growing out of people's own struggles and what really matters to them.

Whether it be the political struggles of Northern Ireland as outlined so powerfully by John Hume or the challenges presented to local culture by the forces of the global culture, we need to be engaging in the debate centred on the values which animate.

The theme, 'Is the Future My Responsibility?', is a follow on from our three previous conferences – 'Are We Forgetting Something?' (1998), 'Working Towards Balance' (1999), and 'Redefining Roles and Relationships' (2000).

We are deeply indebted to the speakers and chairpeople for their valuable contributions and their enthusiasm. Over 600 people from a cross section of Irish society attended. We were particularly delighted that so many young people were among the attendance. Through this publication, we want many more to share the thoughts and aspirations that have emerged from the conference.

We would like to extend our sincerest thanks to our sponsors ESB, Waterford Crystal, Aer Lingus, West County Hotel, Ennis Information Age Town, and Gilbeys. We are grateful for the promotional and publicity work done on behalf of the conference by the Rightword Company. Organisation, teamwork, punctuality and accommodation are vital for a conference to run smoothly. For this, we are grateful to Máire Johnston, Conference Co-ordinator, Céifin and RRD staff, the Conference Committee and the volunteers who gave so generously of their time.

Harry Bohan
February 2002

CONFERENCE INTRODUCTION

Harry Bohan

This particular story started back in 1997 when some of us began to look at the implications of the massive change taking place in Irish society. Initially we did this through reflection and we were assisted in this process through close association with a contemplative order. We initiated our debate through this series of conferences under the broad heading of 'Our Society in the New Millennium'.

In 1998 we asked 'Are We Forgetting Something?' This led us to 'Working Towards Balance' in 1999 and to 'Redefining Roles and Relationships' in 2000. Along the way pertinent questions were posed, such as 'Who is raising the next generation?' We debated 'the breaking of trust' and its implications for society and we were told how we could each use 'our circle of influence' to improve things.

The Céifin International Institute for Values-Led Change has come about directly as a result of these conferences. We know that this Institute is timely and can make a major contribution to understanding societal change leading to personal change and organisational change.

It goes without saying that Ireland has enjoyed a decade of unprecedented economic growth that has brought with it tremendous benefits for the country as a whole. We are currently experiencing a slow-down. That may be no bad thing. It gives us a chance to pause. But we are now a very wealthy country. Technology delivers the marvels that knit our world together. We are at the very heart of the communications revolution. People are not afraid anymore to voice their opinion. Most of us are enjoying a standard of living unheard of a few decades ago.

We are the best fed, best housed, best educated, most employed generation ever to have lived in Ireland. Yes we have problems, with the medical services and traffic for example, but in material terms most of us are well off. However, there are more fundamental challenges facing us and these are to do with meaning to life, with relationships. We hear more and more people talk about the emptiness of modern life, who wonder where meaning is coming from and what values are shaping us. We ask why people have become so aggressive and indeed violent? We have become very aware that life has become devalued. People say it is not easy being young these days in spite of the choices and the freedom.

So we could ask: Have we become helpless in the face of change or can we manage the future? Is it my responsibility at a personal level and at an organisational level? Is it the fact that as the authoritarianism of the past was abandoned at the same time as we experienced extraordinary economic development that there was a loss of nerve in appealing to Church social values?

Professor Joe Lee, one of the previous contributors at our conferences, recently made the statement that 'achieving balance and harmony is now a far more formidable challenge to humankind than achieving perpetual economic growth.' These conferences are an attempt to generate serious debate around these issues and to point the way forward towards reconstructing society around relationships. We now have come to a stage of taking some serious steps that could help.

The major economic change in Ireland was sparked off by massive investment in expanding existing universities and institutes and in establishing new ones during the seventies and eighties. One could say that the Celtic Tiger economy was rooted in education, as a highly educated workforce was responsible in a big way for attracting the massive investment here during the nineties.

As we know, this economic development was and continues to be driven by market values and in one way or another market values have dominated our lives for many years. These market values are central to business and industry. They are competitive and aggressive. However, they can be very inappropriate when applied to other areas of life. They are inappropriate if they over-influence the professions, such as medicine or law, if they are responsible for the exploitation of young people, if they undermine family life, or push the elderly, the weak or the vulnerable to the sidelines.

Side by side with this major economic growth was witnessed an equally huge disengagement by much of the population from the supports and institutions that sustained them for generations. During these years Ireland experienced serious disconnection from family and community and from organisations, both religious and political. Institutions which shaped us are finding it extremely difficult to address a youthful and questioning culture. Exposure to the global culture is intensive due to the mass media revolution, something that is nowhere more evident than in the Irish contribution to the rock music and film industries. We no longer identify with the people, places or structures which gave previous generations an identity and a feeling of belonging. There is a vacuum. In his new book, *The Elephant and Flea*, Charles Handy poses the question, 'Should we be worried by the fact that more of us don't belong to any formal community? Probably. Life without belonging properly to anything, life without commitment, means life without responsibility, to others or for others. The independent life is an invitation to selfishness and a recipe for a very privatised society. But where there is no responsibility for others there is no concept of right or wrong. Do whatever you want, as long as it is within the law, or more realistically, as long as you don't get caught. Maximize your advantage. Why not?'

Is it an exaggeration to suggest that in very many communities our neighbours wouldn't be aware or even care if we were to disappear from among them? As often as not, 'neighbour' in Ireland today means someone with a common address but little more.

The reality is that the market economy does not function as a community. It is a highly competitive environment as distinct from one that depends on relationships. We have invested huge resources in developing the economy. We are now challenged to make a clear distinction between market values and social values, or to at least balance them. We are challenged to reflect on values that will reconnect us, which will value life and relationships. We are called on to invest resources in ensuring that we respond to this challenge. We can not assume that by sitting back and simply commenting that the storm will blow over or that we will return to the old ways. The fact is we are experiencing a cultural transformation, we are witnessing the passing of a tradition, the end of an era.

As Dr Tom Collins previously told us: 'We don't have a history or a language to help us shape the future.' Change has to be managed if we are to take responsibility for our future. Churches, communities, corporations, professions, public services and families all have a part to play, but they must understand change and work out how, if they are to play their part effectively.

Nature does not like a vacuum, but a vacuum is what occurs when people demand freedom without accepting responsibility.

We all know what happens when we have a political vacuum. In the same way a social and spiritual vacuum has to be filled also.

More and more, individuals and communities are being shattered by violence and aggression. We don't have to move outside our own county to know this.

I meet people every day with questions like *'Why aren't they doing something about it?'* or *'Who is responsible for this, that or the other?'* People rarely ask *'Have I got any responsibility for the way things are?'* That is why we have decided, after giving the issue much thought, that the theme of this year's conference should be 'Is The Future My Responsibility?' This is a question we all need to ask and no doubt we will get much food for thought over the next two days.

This country has a powerful tradition of community living. We have a deep spiritual and cultural heritage. The family and community bond held generations together – all of this in times of poverty. In recent times we have made huge strides in resurrecting Irish music and dance. Thanks to people like John Hume we have also made heroic efforts and enormous progress towards attaining peace on this island. We have a strong economy in spite of the current slow down.

We are now challenged to restore social and human values, to restore balance to people's lives. And how can the Céifin Institute help? Céifin is not about changing the world. It is about listening to people and engaging with organisations to facilitate an understanding of change and to find ways and means of shaping the future. It is about reflecting on values and applying theory to practice. We believe that in the same way that we required new universities and institutes for technological and economic development we now require an institute that will address the human, social and spiritual issues facing Ireland today. We now require an institute that will help restore the balance that is so obviously lacking.

While it will be some time before the actual Céifin building will be in place, the work of Céifin has already begun. We already have a group reflecting on values and how these can be applied in a changing society. We have a Corporate Network contemplating values in the workplace. We have research programmes dealing with the family and with work and lifestyle either already up and running or in the pipeline.

Primarily, this Institute is about providing a focal point for research and reflection, for sharing and for reaching out to where people are, where they live and work. It is about facilitating corporations, professions, policy makers, churches, families and communities to respond to the needs of our time.

This conference and the Céifin Institute are all about getting involved in an understanding of this changed society and finding ways and means of shaping the future.

WHY IS THE FUTURE MY RESPONSIBILITY?

John Hume, MEP

Thank you all for having me here this evening to address this conference. As you are aware, of course, this conference is built around a question: Is the future my responsibility? The simple answer to that question, as you would all agree, is Yes. But in developing that answer I believe it is important that we address the more fundamental question, which is, *why* is the future my responsibility? And I am reminded this evening of the words of Charles Kettering, who once said, 'My interest is in the future, because I am going to spend the rest of my life there.' As you all are. And how right he was. Because the future, or more appropriately, what type of future it is we wish to live in, is the single most important question now facing our country, indeed the entire world. It is something that should engage us all, because our actions today will have real and direct consequences for our children and for future generations. And for that very reason, I feel that it is crucial that we, in this country, at this particular time, should opt to seek out new and better political paths to follow. I am talking particularly about the Northern part now. In doing so, to leave behind the outdated politics of confrontation and of bigotry and to leave it where it belongs, in the past.

Let us build a new future together. We owe it to ourselves and to each other but even more so we owe it to future generations. Having experienced our past, we owe it to them to create a new society in which diversity is a source of strength and not a source of division, in which difference is respected and not fought about. As many of you would know perhaps, I am a very strong advocate of European Union for very many reasons. The European Union is not merely an economic tool or a social tool or a tool for cultural change – it is of course all of those, but at its very heart lies the philosophy that, in my opinion, contains the key to conflict resolution in every corner of the world, the blueprint for developing the full potential of diversity, and respect for diversity and difference, which is central to peace in the world.

The century we have just left was the worst in the history of the world with two world wars in the first half of it. By 1945, Europe appeared to be totally divided, millions of people were dead. People in 1945 had just emerged from the second bloody and bitter world war of that century. In my own town – I was a child at the time – we had to go out and live in what we called 'air-raid shelters'. Part of our city was bombed. The principles of respect, of tolerance, of partnership, and the development of common economic interest, in those days, appeared to be unobtainable. Yet, within a few years, the understanding that human beings cannot live apart prevailed, and today the European Union stands as a most vibrant testimony to the ideal that we are all better working with each other and for each others.

I have to tell you that the European Union has been a very powerful inspiration to the development of my own philosophy. I always tell the story of when I was first elected to the European Parliament in Strasbourg in 1979. I went there and I went for a walk and I walked across the bridge from Strasbourg in France to Kiel in Germany because they are that close. I stopped in the middle and I meditated. I thought: Good Lord, 1979, if I had stood on this bridge thirty years ago in 1949 when the Second World War had just ended and thirty five million people had been slaughtered for the second time in a century, and said then, 'Don't worry, in thirty years time we will be all together, united, and the French will still be French and the German will still be German', I would have been sent to a psychiatrist. But it has happened and, therefore, it is the duty of everyone, in every area of conflict, to study how and why it happened, because it is the best example in the history of the world of conflict resolution.

The principles at the heart of the European Union, in my opinion, are principles that will solve conflict, and when you study it, you will find that they are also the principles at the heart of the Good Friday Agreement in the North. Principle number one: respect for difference, no victory for either side. Principle number two: institutions that respect the differences, a Council of Ministers from all countries, a European Commission from all countries and a European Parliament from all countries. And principle number three: most important of all, working together in their common interests and breaking down the barriers of centuries. The new Europe has evolved and is still evolving. That lesson is there for all areas of conflict.

At the end of the day, if you stop and think, if you are forced to, if you have lived through what we have lived through over the last thirty years, and watched one out of five hundred people in the North lose their lives, and one out of fifty being maimed and injured, you have to think not only how can we stop this, but how can we give the same philosophy to people elsewhere who might be suffering? Because all conflict is about the same thing, no matter where it is – it is about difference, whether the difference is your race, your religion or your nationality. The answer to difference, therefore, is to respect it. As I often say, difference is an accident of birth – none of us chose to be born; we didn't choose to be born into any nationality, any religion or any race. Therefore, it is not something that we should fight about. It is something we should respect. Difference is of the essence of humanity – there are not two people in this room who are the same. There are not two people in the whole human race who are the same. Therefore, we should respect difference and create societies in which diversity is respected and which understand that this is the very essence of unity. This is a deep lesson for this country. Unity is not about one side defeating or taking over another. It is about real respect for difference and it is one from which I won't waver because I think it is the right course of action.

What we have seen in the North is the greatest tragedy of a generation, and the people of Ireland, all of us, have lived through it. The disastrous consequences of people not facing up to their responsibilities for the future, the terror and tragedy of the Troubles, we have all endured the bloodshed and suffering and the terrible political inertia in facing up to the problem. But we have also seen the unquenchable hope encapsulated by ordinary people who lived through it. As I said in my Nobel Peace Prize speech in 1998, 'Amid shattered lives, a quiet heroism has borne silent rebuke to the evil that violence represents, to the carnage and waste of violence and to its ultimate futility.' Violence has no part to play in the future of our country. It has played a terrible part in our history and, in so doing, it has undermined each generation's chances to shape their future in new and exciting ways. I have always been and always will oppose violence. I was very heavily inspired in my early days by the philosophy of Martin Luther King when I was one of the early members of the civil rights movement in Northern Ireland. Of course, throughout the seventies, eighties and nineties, I stood in total opposition to all of the violence, naturally, and indeed when I engaged in dialogue with Gerry

Adams. Our joint statement made clear that the objective of our dialogue was to bring violence to an end.

Since then another organisation has emerged, calling itself the Real IRA, perpetrating the worst atrocity of the past three decades by killing twenty-nine people and two unborn children in one day in Omagh. Yes, we are not only opposed to it today, we are opposed to it tomorrow and the next day and all days because it has no place at all in society. The people behind it must come to realise that their day is over and they must also realise that, despite whatever philosophies they have been handed down from the past, it is the people of this island that are divided, not the territory. And when people are divided, what does violence do? It deepens the division and makes the problem more difficult to solve. And nobody using it can claim to be seeking human rights because they are undermining the most fundamental human right of all – the right to life.

We must work to replace all of that with hope. We must concentrate on addressing the real issues that face our society – real politics – poverty, unemployment, poor quality housing, low standards in health care, roads, real human rights, real standards of living, so that we can pray in Ireland that our young people can, at last, all earn a living in the land of their birth.

My first political lesson came when I was ten years old in Derry. The Nationalist Party was holding, as it did in those years, an election meeting on the streets, with loudspeakers on the backs of lorries. I was standing with my father, who was unemployed. They were whooping up emotions and waving the flags, and I was getting emotional too. My father put his hand on my shoulder and said, 'Listen son, don't you go getting involved in that stuff.' I said, 'Why not Dad?' He said, 'You can't eat a flag.' Think of the wisdom of that. The political parties that use the national flag as their emblem are undermining the value of it because it is supposed to represent the unity of the people of the country and if political parties use it as they do in the North it becomes very divisive. I have always believed that through tackling the issues that matter to the people in their day-to-day lives we can find the common ground that will unite our people. Waving the flag is waving two different colours at one another.

Of the three principles at the heart of the European Union and the Good Friday Agreement, the third principle is the most important – working together in our common interests, what I call the healing process. Now that our institutions are in place, the public representatives from the different sections of the community and between North and South will be working together. And as they do that, we will then be spilling our sweat not our blood, breaking down the barriers of the past distrust by working the common ground together, the real healing process. The real border in this country is not a line on a map, it is in the minds and the hearts of people, and that border cannot be removed by victory of one side over another. It can only be removed by the healing process that builds the trust, that breaks down the barriers of mistrust over centuries and by working together we will do that.

Just as the new Europe has evolved, the dream and hope is that the new Ireland will evolve based on agreement and respect for difference. And it will be real unity if it is a united people based on agreement. You are not united if it is not agreed and you have a divided people, then the quarrel continues. Real unity, and of course, unity through republicanism involving Catholic, Protestant and Dissenter, means living together in equality and harmony. I listen to some people calling themselves Republicans, talking about uniting Ireland with guns and bombs, but how can you unite Catholics, Protestants and Dissenters with a gun and a bomb? Will we please at last learn that lesson, because it is taking a long time to do so?

I believe, also, through the creation of new employment and new opportunities, and working in real politics in this country, North and South, that our young people will be given a new lease of hope. I want to live, and I am sure that you do too, in an Ireland that is at work, an Ireland in which our young people can participate in the highest possible standards of training and education, have decent jobs, and live in the land of their birth. The tide of emigration may have turned over the past ten years, but the imperative is to create a rising tide of prosperity and opportunity that will lift our communities out of disadvantage and into employment, that will breathe new life into our cities, our towns and our rural areas. I want the people of Ireland to focus on creating a better future for us all and for our young people in particular.

In March 1982, I was delivering the same speech to two different audiences in two churches in Belfast – one Protestant and one Catholic – on consecutive evenings. I pointed out that many people in Northern Ireland had a compulsive desire to live in the past; nearly all the slogans about politics were about the past – remember 1690, remember this, remember that. I said then that we all have a choice whether or not to indulge in an endless sterile exchange of 'whataboutery'. 'What about' was the most favoured phrase in elections, starting with the outrage that suits us – you know, what about the outrages of violent men? What about the sectarian murders? What about discrimination? What about 1912? What about 1916? What about 1689, the siege of Derry? What about 1641? And so on. Each 'what about' being used to justify another tragedy. And to claim credit for it, another 'what about'. Let us instead now ask ourselves just one question – what about the future?

The Good Friday Agreement has provided us all with that opportunity to leave the past behind and to focus on building a new and agreed Ireland. We must take that chance and we must take it now. It is our best hope for a future of peace, of hope and of opportunity. It is our absolute responsibility to deliver that Agreement in its entirety. It is your Agreement, and the most historic thing to happen in that Agreement, and I am very happy that it was myself that proposed it, is that when the

Agreement is reached the last word would be with the people and not the politicians. And the people of Ireland as a whole came out in strength and ninety per cent of people in the South voted 'yes' for that Agreement, and seventy-two per cent in the North. So for the first time in our history, the people of Ireland had spoken of how they wished to live together and, for that reason, none of the violent organisations can now claim, as they always have done, that they are seeking the self-determination of the Irish people.

It is the duty of all true democrats to implement the will of the people and that is what is now happening. The institutions, are now bedding down, the process of decommissioning of weapons has begun, and the new Police Service of Northern Ireland has begun its work. It is a time of change and a time of challenge, but I believe the Pro-Agreement parties are ready to lead the community through those changes and meet those challenges, and we in the North owe deep gratitude to the leaders of the parties in the Dáil who have put peace in our land at the top of their agenda. I am certain today that the outlook for our future is brighter than it has been before.

Ireland can become a great place to live and to grow in the new century and the new millennium. We are duty-bound to make sure it does. We are living through two of the biggest revolutions in the history of the world – the technological telecommunications and transport revolutions – which have made the world a much smaller place, and that strengthens our ability because we are one of the wandering peoples in the world, as you know, because of emigrations of the past. There are seventy million people today across the world of Irish descent. Now that we are living in a smaller world we can harness that strength. As I have said often in speeches in the South, I would like to see the Government of the Republic issuing a certificate of Irish identity to people all over the world who are of Irish descent. Think of the strength that would bring to our little island, in economic terms alone. Just imagine if every one of them only spent ten euro a week on something Irish? Think of the strength that would give us in influencing the world and helping the smaller world, particularly the Third World, the countries that are suffering terribly from deprivation and starvation. We could not only be sending to such countries money and food, which is only part-time assistance, but real help that will help them stand on their own feet. The best thing you can do for any people is make sure that they have a full-scale system of education, to the highest level, open to all sections of the people. The only wealth we have is human beings. Without human beings any piece of earth is only a jungle. It is human beings who create, and the more equipped they are to create the more they will do it. It is education that does this and when the history of this country is studied you will discover that the economic regeneration really began when education was provided and the people, the young people, took advantage of that and became the creators. And, as I say, we can help the smaller world and the Third World a lot. Because of the Diaspora we can become a very important people in that world.

I cannot state my opposition to racism and bigotry strongly enough. As I have said earlier, it is an accident of birth what we are born and where we are born and we shouldn't be fighting about it. We should be respecting it. And Ireland, I hope, in the new century and the new millennium, will be multi-cultural and dynamic and will have true unity of Catholic, Protestant and Dissenter. In the North, I hope that our framework will develop the potential of diversity that can be applied to the island as a whole. I want to live, and I am sure you do too, in an Ireland that is caring, an Ireland which takes care of our most vulnerable and the most weak in our society and does not ignore them – real politics. An Ireland which is safe and free and happy – real politics. I want to live in an Ireland which is tackling poverty as our first and last priority. And let me ask you: is it right that a single person in our society should be allowed to live in poverty? Is it right that anyone should be homeless? Is it right that children should be hungry? These are all realities facing society today. These are the challenges that face us today – the challenge of real politics. Not eating flags. Tackling the social and economic needs of the people means working the common ground that unites our people, and that's what we should do.

I hope, and I am determined to do my part with my party, that the challenges of today will become the successes of tomorrow. This is my wish for the future. I know that perhaps it may be ambitious given our recent past, but when ambition, determination and vision all cross each other, anything is possible, and I am confident that we in Ireland can face into the future, a future that is, indeed, all of our responsibility, with real confidence and real conviction. And the creation here of Céifin, an institute for values-led change, is ideal, both in its timing and in its philosophy. The revolution we are living through, particularly in telecommunications and television, has undermined the sense of neighbourhood, the sense of community, and stopped a lot of communication, but organisations of this nature can naturally redevelop the community interests of the past.

I always tell of when I was a child growing up on our streets. We didn't have television, we all walked to school together, nobody had cars, we all walked back together, we played games in the streets together, our parents went next door and sat having cups of tea and chatting to one another – communication was normal all the time. That has been reduced abnormally by the telecommunications world. Parents don't even, much of the time, talk to their children; they are all sitting watching television. One main objective of this institute, which I feel is very visionary, is to restore that kind of work, that type of society where communities become communities again and where we meet regularly and discuss our common problems and our common enjoyments. And I hope the existence of a movement such as this will concentrate our minds on the challenges that lie ahead of us at community level and at national level. Let us hope that very soon in this new century we will have a new Ireland and that the principles that build it can also be taken to other areas of conflict in the world and that we can, at last, have centuries and millenniums where there are no conflicts and no wars and where human beings respect their common humanity.

THE NEW WORLD OF ELEPHANTS AND FLEAS

Charles Handy

It is a great pleasure to share a platform with John Quinn. He is a special man, a special friend. And at last I have been able to get to Ennis and meet the legendary Harry Bohan. Thank you, Father, for inviting me, it is a great privilege to be here.

It is good, too, to be back in the land of my birth again. I left Ireland forty-odd years ago. It was a dark land then. It seemed to be a land without much hope, fixated with its past. So it has been very exciting coming back these last ten years. To see the signs of economic progress – the cranes, the traffic jams, the road works, the smog, the queues at the restaurants, the prices on the menus, the housing. Those things do, alas, go with progress but I would agree that Ireland has never had it so good. If it was like this now, I wouldn't have left forty years ago. But I am still disappointed because I had hoped, or maybe I can still hope, that Ireland, as a late entry into the capitalist world, might actually get it right, might somehow avoid the terrible inequities, the inequalities that you find in some places in America, for instance.

Did you know that in America's boom years in the 1990s thirty per cent of Americans actually saw their incomes decline? They don't tell you that, do they? Did you know that another fifty per cent stayed the same? So to keep up with the aspirational levels, with everybody having it so good, you would have to have two people working their guts out whereas, in their parents generation, one would have been enough. They are working harder to stay still. Do you not think it is a little obscene that in the top five hundred corporations in America the chief executives earn on average four hundred and sixty times the take home pay of the people at the bottom of their organisations?

It is not as bad as that in Ireland but there are still too many poor people. And I had hoped that you would avoid the trap of the *chindogu*. *Chindogu* is a Japanese word. It is what the Japanese use to describe unnecessary things. My favourite example is windscreen wipers for your spectacles, for when you go out in the rain. Christmas is a *chindogu* festival these days. The problem of *chindogu* is that with economic growth, once we have got all we need in society, then economic growth seems to depend on more and more *chindogu*. Stuff that we don't really need but we are persuaded to want by those clever people in the advertising world, all those alluring displays in the shopping malls. I walked through a shopping mall in Dublin two days ago, there really wasn't anything I needed, quite a few things I wanted, but I didn't need them.

Now isn't it odd that our economic growth depends on producing more and more things that we don't need, so that we can pay more and more people to do work to produce these useless things. I am not clever enough to know the solution, but it seems odd to me that we cannot make money and wealth out of good things like better health, better education, better environment, but instead we have to produce more *chindogu* in order to pay for those things. I hope that Ireland can solve the *chindogu* problem. But anyway, you now have a chance to solve the next problem of capitalism, which is this: the looming fragility, insecurity and frailty of our organisations, not just those in business, all our large organisations. At the same time, and partly as a consequence, we are seeing the rise of the autonomous individual. That double happening is what I mean by the elephants and the fleas.

This is a serious problem. These large organisations have been the pillars of our society. The last century was the century of the organisation – most people worked in them. That is where they got their money; that is where they spent their days, at least one member of each family; that was how the State collected their taxes; that is how the State made sure that every family had an income coming in, with just a few people who weren't in an organisation getting some kind of dole out; that is how the State made sure we were all protected from dangerous machines and so on; that is how many people in some countries got their health care paid for – through the organisation. If those elephants start going weak at the knees we will be removing one of the props of our society. Yet that is what is happening.

Let me give you some statistics. Peter Drucker says that about 40 per cent of the people who work for and with organisations these days are not employed by them, they are outside. They are what I call the fleas – small organisations, individuals, partnerships, on some kind of contract arrangement, but not employed by the organisation. Let me put it another way around. If you look at the working force in Great Britain, and I imagine it is probably much the same in Ireland, only 40 per cent of the workforce in Great Britain today has what they call an indefinite period contract, that is, the kind of rolling contract where you cannot get sacked without three months' notice. So if you are in a proper job with a proper contract in an organisation these days, you are in a minority.

There are probably more elephants represented here than fleas, but I think it is going to change. For one thing, you are going to live for a longer time, perhaps into your eighties, unless you smoke too much or drive too fast. And you will be out of that elephant increasingly in your late fifties, early sixties, if not sooner. And I am afraid to say that you won't be as rich as you would have hoped to be, pensions everywhere in the developed world are not going to be adequate, because nobody expected people to live that long. You will want to work a bit but won't have a proper job after you are fifty-five or sixty. For about twenty years you will be a part-time flea. So get ready!

Furthermore, a lot of young people find that they need to alternate a little bit of work and a little bit of study these days, and they flit about from organisation to organisation, quite sensibly, trying themselves out, finding where they fit, so it will be 'fleadom' at the beginning and end of life as well as, for many, in the middle. Let me now list the types of flea – just to make sure you know what I am talking about. There are five types: first, there are the 'in-house revolutionaries'. These are the mavericks; elephants need to be scratched under the armpits, otherwise they get a little bit staid and dull. They need to be made dance a little. All organisations need these people and they need to give them space and allow them to experiment and, if need be, to be different from the norms.

Then there are the 'professional and expert fleas', people who call themselves consultants, accountants, lawyers, whatever, the people now who are increasingly outside the organisation. Why keep a lawyer in-house when maybe for half the time he is not needed? Why not call him in when you need him? More and more people are like that. In fact, organisations are increasingly putting their best people outside because it is too expensive to keep them inside. Think, for instance, of my publisher, Random House, the biggest publisher in the British Isles. This organisation depends entirely on the intellectual property provided by its authors – people like me, or, more importantly, John Grisham, who solely boosted the profits of

Random House by 30 per cent last year. Their authors are their most important assets, yet none of those people are actually employed by Random House.

Can you think of any other organisation that has all its assets outside the organisation, not inside. But that is the way they work in publishing. Basically, it is too expensive for them to employ John Grisham, and if they employed John Grisham and guaranteed him five million pounds a year salary, there is just a thought that he might not do any work for it! It's quite risky, and quite expensive, so they push their intellectual property outside and make them into independent fleas. More and more organisations are eventually going to do that with their human assets.

Then there are the 'entrepreneurial fleas', people who create businesses and build organisations, and I'll talk a little more about that shortly. There are the 'occasional fleas', the people at the beginning and end of life and, finally, there are the 'reluctant fleas', those who are pushed out of the elephants as redundant.

The dilemma for the elephants is the inexorable formula they have to work to, which I first came across some years ago. A company chairman told me the secret of his company's success, or what would be, if he could make it work. He said, 'in five years time, sooner if possible, I want to have half as many people employed by my company working twice as hard, producing three times as much – a half times two times three in short.' That is wonderful if you are the half that stays, even though you are now working harder – sixty-five hours a week for some of you no doubt. But what about the other half, the half that has to go? Some of them are professional fleas but a lot are reluctant fleas. The companies have to follow that formula because the pressure of competition in a globalised world is intense, it never ever stops. Just when you think you have got it right, someone else comes along who has done it cheaper.

The situation is made worse by the threat of the new invaders. Seven years ago I had the privilege of addressing the booksellers in Killarney. What they were worried about was competition from America, from Barnes and Nobles and Borders, big chains of booksellers in America, rumoured to be invading Britain and then Ireland. But actually the real invader would also come from America although they had never heard of him. He was a guy called Geoff Bezos, who was sitting in his parents' home, dreaming up a little thing called Amazon.com. He wasn't a bookseller at all; he was just a whiz kid with an idea from the new technology. It is called a disruptive technology, because it changes everything in its sector.

Competition comes out of a clear blue sky these days. My own company, Shell, now 110 years old, had been spending fortunes over the years building up their brand. Two years ago, they woke up in Britain to discover that the main seller of petrol in Britain was Tesco, a grocer! Not Mobil, not Esso, or Texaco, but Tesco. So here was this special brand that they had developed and with which they hoped to be sold at a premium price while the same product was being sold as a loss loser along with eggs and milk. Shell hadn't noticed what was happening because Tesco wasn't a traditional competitor. As a result, everybody who sells petrol in Britain, including Shell, loses money. They have to sell the stuff otherwise they couldn't make money on the refining and the digging to get the oil. So they go back to this formula, a half times two times three, and they cut the staff, and cut the costs.

The economists call it increased productivity and I call it shedding fleas, which doesn't sound as proper. Yet that is the truth, it is shedding fleas. And it is going to go on and on and on. You may say that it's only once or twice because of the recession. No, I promise you it isn't the recession. It was going to happen anyway, because of the relentless pressure of competition. And in fact, the more the economy grows, the more competition you get.

The elephants have another problem. Their assets are no longer in their buildings and their machines. Their assets are the heads and hearts of the people who work there. Karl Marx got it right in the end. He said, 'The workers would win when they owned the means of production'. Well, of course, he meant that they would own the factories. It hasn't worked out like that but they do own the means of production in their heads and in their hearts, in their skills, their knowledge and their experience. These are very tricky assets to manage. They can walk away. If they are talented enough they can go where they want, they can step outside and be a flea. Twenty years ago Peter Drucker said that the problem of managing the knowledge worker would be that they would want more than livelihood from their work, more than just money. They want a reason; they want a purpose; they want a cause. And I have to tell you, you don't jump out of the bed in the morning wanting to make the shareholders rich – not even if you are a shareholder yourself. You want to feel that you are doing something useful for the world.

Organisations, the elephants, really have to rethink: what are they there for, over and above keeping their shareholders happy? If you are an elephant, answer me this: why do you exist? If you did not exist, would we invent you? Because you are important, you really are. We fleas need you and society needs you because you deliver the goods. But we want to know what you are doing for the world. Please boast about it because otherwise you will get yourself a bad name. People will just think you are selfish. It is not a game. It should be a cause.

Now, for those of you who will be fleas, and all those of you who are fleas, I have some challenges. I have to tell you that your future is increasingly your responsibility. I never thought it was to be honest. When I left my college I applied for a job with Shell, the oil company. When I got it I wrote back to my mother and father in Ireland and I said 'life is solved'. Because I really thought that Shell was responsible for my future, as they said they were. They even drew a line on a graph showing me my typical life, a line that I was glad to see went up. Then I married Elizabeth after about eight years. Elizabeth said to me, 'Do you know what you have just done? You have just handed over your life to people that you haven't really met, to a corporation. They are going to tell you what to do and where to go and what to learn and what success is. Did you mean to do that?' And I said yes. But as I said it I realised what a strange thing it was to have done, to sign away my life to a corporation.

I didn't become totally free and totally independent until I was forty-nine; I should have done it earlier, but at forty-nine I set out to be a writer. Unfortunately, I didn't have a publisher and I had only written one book. So life was a bit scary, but I believed that I had it in me. So, when you start as a flea, and I promise you that you all will, you have to decide what you have got inside you that you can turn into something useful. I believe, however, that we all have hidden things inside us that we are not always aware of, things that can transform our lives.

Let me tell you the story of Johnny W. Johnny W. is a friend of mine who is an advertising executive, and he came to see me, and he said, 'Charles, it is terrible. I am forty-eight, in the prime of life, and I have just been made redundant by my advertising firm. Can you find me another job?' and I said, 'Johnny, what can you do?' 'Well,' he said, 'I am an advertising executive, I do advertising.' I said, 'Yes, but that is no use, you are too old for that world. What else can you do?' He said, 'I've never done anything else, I am an advertising executive, that is all I can do.' I said, 'Do this for me: go to twenty people who know you personally, at work or at home, and ask them to tell you one thing that you are good at, not an analysis of your life, not a list of your strengths and weaknesses, just one thing you are good at.' He said, very reluctantly, that he would do as I asked. He came back in two weeks and he said, 'I have got this amazing list of twenty things, but, strangely, nobody mentioned advertising executive!'

But of course they said other things such as 'you are very good at getting groups to work together', 'you are very good at presenting things', 'you are very good at encouraging creativity in people' and so on, and so forth. He can now put these things together in a different package and find a totally different way of presenting himself to the world and a different way of earning money. There were things inside him he did not know about. Sometimes, you actually need a shock to bring those things out.

This happened to Dee Dawson. Dee studied in the London Business School under me when I was there, for an MBA. A year after she finished she came back. 'I have made a great mistake,' she said. 'I don't want to be a businesswoman, I want to be a doctor.' She was thirty-three years old with three children so it was going to be difficult, but I wrote her a letter of reference and she got in. After seven years and two more kids she qualified. There she was with an MBA and a doctor's degree so she went off for a holiday with her husband in the South of France to celebrate. He had supported her in the meantime with a software consulting firm back in London. During the holiday he flew back to see how his business was and discovered that his colleagues had stolen it all – the computer, the files, the customers and the money. He broke down. So there she was with a broken husband, five kids, and no money. 'What have I got?' She asked herself. 'I've got five kids. I know about kids. I have a medical degree, a business degree and a big house.' So she shoved all the kids into one room and opened the first private anorexic clinic in Britain. None of this had she planned on before the disaster to her husband's firm. You don't know what you have got in you until you need it.

Dee Dawson was one of the 'new alchemists' that Elizabeth and I studied some three years ago. We called them alchemists because they created something out of nothing, something that every flea may need to do, to find the gap in the market where their talent can fit. You could call our alchemists 'super fleas'. We believed that we could learn something from their examples that would be relevant to more ordinary fleas. What was it, we wondered, that gave these people the ability to dare to make something out of nothing, something that no-one else had done?

There were two principle things in their backgrounds, we found. First of all, these people cared. They had passion. They were making a dream come true. If you have passion for something, you can endure anything. You can learn anything, because you want to. And you can persevere, because the first two years of any venture are tough – you don't make very much money, you are worried, and you work too hard.

Secondly, the alchemists have great self-belief. Not only do they have passion, they knew they could deliver. And how did they get that self belief? Nearly all of them, in some way or another, in the first twenty-four years of their life, had been given a 'golden seed' by someone – that is what Freud called it. Somebody had said to them, somebody they respected, 'I have been watching you, you are incredibly talented as an artist'; or 'You are going to be a brilliant teacher'; or 'I can see how well you relate to people'; or 'you are a clever marketing man; you know about customers!' It had to be someone they respected. They tucked this seed away but never forgot it. When I told Dee Dawson, the one who wanted to be a doctor, that she might not be clever enough to pass her medical exams, she said, 'You are wrong Charles. When I did my A-Level biology, my biology teacher told me I got the best grade in the whole region. So I know that I am clever!' Twelve years before, that teacher had given her this golden seed and she had never forgotten.

Somebody, somewhere, at some time, will have given each of you a golden seed. You may not have watered it, so let it come out – this hidden thing inside you – and dream. And the dream will lead you to your passion. Oh, and by the way, if you do nothing else after this conference, please give someone a golden seed, before the end of the year. They must deserve it of course. Don't cast your seeds on stony ground – they won't take root. It is the greatest gift a teacher can give, the greatest gift a boss can give, the greatest gift an uncle, a godfather, an aunt can give, or, of course, a parent.

Elizabeth and I were invited in September to Geneva to meet with a hundred so-called 'global leaders' of tomorrow, by the World Economic Forum. They had selected one hundred people under the age of thirty five as the people most likely to succeed and lead in their profession. They weren't all businessmen, some were, but there were doctors, scientists, writers, community workers, whatever, from all over the world – all colours, all creeds, all languages. We went with some misgivings, thinking we were going to meet a lot of egotistical yuppies, and we were amazed. Because these people were both successful and impressive. They had reached what I call 'the second level of success'. In other words, they had already proved themselves at an early age. They had reached the first level of success, and now they were on the second level. And on the second level they did not want to do that again. They actually wanted to leave a footprint in the sand of time. To do something that mattered. They were free to dream, to find their passion.

As a flea, I discovered, I was also free.

When I used to work for Shell, I had sold them all my time, I had given them all my working life and the only question was how much money they were going to give me for that time. Anyone who is in an organisation wants more money for the time that they have already sold. But now you leave the organisation and become a flea. You can make more money as a flea if you work more hours. But you could decide to work less hours and make less money. There is a trade off, which there never had been before. So now you can say, 'If I want more time and a better balance in my life, how much money do I actually need, not want, but need?' And, actually, the lower you set your need, or define 'enough', the more freedom you have to do other things, if you wanted to. Then you have to work out what enough is.

Elizabeth and I decided that since I was swamping her life with my work, we would divide our year in two. I would have six months, the winter months to do my work. She would manage me in those months, and would have the summer months when the light was better to do her photography, and I would hold the umbrellas and carry cameras, and drive her. But the problem is that, as a result, we both split our earnings in half. Could we risk it in order to be together all the time? And we decided that at our age we could do that. As you get older you need less money and then you are freer to do what you want. So you do have this trade off, the choice, once you are a flea.

But then you have to say, 'Well what is it all about? What is this time for? You have to get philosophical, religious, in a way? What is it all about? That becomes very difficult to answer. In Shell, I did not have to think about that. They were making and marketing oil. That was their purpose and mine. Now, as a flea, I had to work out my own purpose in life. That becomes very exciting.

But the challenge for society is the following: lots of fleas are reluctant fleas. There are also incompetent fleas, ageing fleas and young fleas. They don't know all these things, they are not super-fleas like the alchemists, they need agents. I have an agent, Elizabeth, and she is exceptionally good. But not everybody is married to an agent. We need agents to help the reluctant fleas particularly. I have been trying to persuade the unions to act as agents, to provide people with help and assistance, to fix their prices, to give them the legal contracts and all else that they need. I have been trying to persuade the employment organisations, the recruitment firms and so forth, to act as employers of first resort. As intermediary employers they should, I suggest, employ people and sell them on. So that they belong somewhere; someone is interested in them; they have a workplace home to go to.

Next, I want a second stream of education. We expect teachers to do too much. Teachers do what teachers can do. They teach you skills and valuable knowledge, but they don't teach you to be a flea; it's not in the curriculum and maybe it shouldn't be in the schools. They don't teach you how to work with different groups of people to solve problems. They don't teach you how to manage your own money. They don't teach you how to sell yourself or how to find what talent you have and to make the most of it, how to turn it into a business or profession. That is not their job. That is why I want to have a parallel stream of education, one that is run by the community, for young people, because they cannot learn early enough that life is not just a set of little hurdles that you jump over and get more grades, and then you join another institution, another elephant and so on and on.

It is not like that anymore. We have to help them. Otherwise, we are deceiving them – we say to them that if you pass all these grades and get all these exams, you will get into the next institution, secondary school or university and then you can go to the next institution which is a work elephant. But the elephants are not going to be there or will only be so for a short time and then the young will get lost, because they have not been prepared for 'fleadom'. We need to prepare people for fleadom in the real world. And we need a new system of words and heroes; unemployment and redundancy, for example, these are awful words. I have tried to substitute a few, like portfolios and portfolio careers, which sound a little more respectable. To say 'I am a portfolio person' sounds better than 'I have just been sacked and don't know what to do'.

We need more words like that that are respectable. Richard Sennett, an American, has written a book called *The Corrosion of Character* about the world he sees is coming, which is a world of independent, selfish individuals. A world without commitment, where people take no responsibility for anything; where the young won't even get married because it is risky. A world where you don't have kids, because they might be a financial burden, and so on. No commitment, certainly not to organisations, a selfish world. I can see a bit of that in society today, but it doesn't have to be that way.

The last time I gave a talk in Dublin I quoted a Chinese proverb, a recipe for happiness; it said: 'Happiness is having something to work on, a project, something to hope for, a dream, and someone to love.' I met someone the other day who had been at that talk, and he said, 'I went out to lunch after it with two people and it was a very depressing lunch because neither of them was in a relationship. They felt that nobody loved them so they weren't going to be happy. And I said, "You don't have to confine love to your sexual partner, you can love all sorts of people. Oh, and by the way, the proverb said *someone to love* – active, not someone to love you."' Give before you receive. If other people don't matter to you, you won't matter to them. But they have to matter first before you matter to them. It is an active verb not a passive one: someone to love, something to hope for and something to work on.

And then just in case you are depressed at the thought of all those super fleas and you say, 'Well, I could never do that. Most people are not like that – most people are ordinary,' then think about these words from John Masefield:

I have seen flowers come in stony places,
And kind things done by men with ugly faces,
And the gold cup won by the worst horse in the race,
And I trust too.

In other words, who knows what you can do in the world of the fleas and even in the world of the elephants, *if* you care enough. Thank you very much.

Question Time

John Quinn, who chaired this session, put some of the questions submitted by the audience to Charles Handy

John Quinn
You mention the need for a second stream of education for people to learn about 'fleadom'. Could you say more about how that might be done? You mention the importance of taking responsibility for our own future. Comment on how formal education encourages/discourages enables/disables them? What do you say to say to parents and young people now leaving school and college without a portfolio yet and who psychologically expect and believe in the elephant but don't know how to be fleas?

Charles Handy
I think the first thing is to start conditioning people to a life that might actually not be in the elephant, at least to start with. I said to our kids when they were young, 'When you leave school or college, don't look for a job.' They would look at me and say, 'Are you that liberal Dad? Do you mean I can just lie around and get the dole?' And I said, 'No, no. I have got to finish the sentence. Don't look for a job, look for a customer, because if you can find someone who will pay you money for something you can do for them or make for them, you will feel so good about yourself. Furthermore, if you do want to look for a job they will be bored stiff with all your grades and they will say, "tell me something that you have actually done", and you will be able to give them something.'

While we are at school we need to prepare people to look for customers. In other words, they have got to have something that they can sell to those customers. I was chairman for a time in the early eighties of a campaign called Education for Capability, in which we said, yes, knowledge and skills are very important, but we also need the ability to work with people, co-operation, to be able to create something and to solve problems, the ability to cope with difficulties on your own, without asking for help from authority, and the capability just to be able to look after yourself. We tried to introduce this into the ordinary school curriculum by persuading people to teach history in this way, or to teach science in this way, but it really was too difficult.

But I remember going to a private boarding school in the South of England and talking about Education for Capability, (this was to the staff). At the end the headmaster, said, 'Well, I think, Charles, that you would probably disapprove of much that we do in the classroom which is really drilling in a sense, but I think you would like all that we do outside the classroom, which are to do with sports, the arts, work experience and going into the community, where they are working with adults, when they are still young.' I said, 'Right, absolutely, the trouble is that you are a very privileged private school. Most people in the State system don't have that chance and they ought to have that chance.'

That is where I want to have the alternative faculty to come in. I left school with this message burned into my mind, that every problem in the world had already been solved but only the teacher knew the answer. The object of the schooling was to get what the teacher knew into my head. Now that is fine and that got me through exams, but then I went out into the world and I still applied that, so when I met something I couldn't solve, I went for the expert. I went up to my boss or to a consultant. Of course, everybody thought that I was pathetic – couldn't do anything on his own, couldn't take initiative – because it never occurred to me that there were lots of problems in the world that I could solve on my own.

That is why I say that, sometimes, we are educated to incompetence and incapacity in our rather rigorous schools. I don't want to change the schools because we do need to teach the people the drills, as it were, but I do want to add onto it in some way, that is where I want the community to help. I believe the British Government are considering reducing the school-leaving age to fourteen; not saying you should leave school at fourteen, but that you can spend part of the week, perhaps two afternoons, perhaps one day, outside the school, outside the classroom in the community.

John Quinn
Would Charles Handy like to comment on the relevance of Dean Swift's dictum, 'Big Fleas have little fleas upon their backs to bite them, and little fleas have lesser fleas and so *ad infinitum*?' Can a group of fleas merge to form an elephant?

Charles Handy
There is an appropriate size for organisations, depending a little on the technology. The appropriate size for Boeing is quite big, you really cannot make aeroplanes without having some big organisation, somewhere. But interestingly, even Boeing is put together with lots of parts of littler firms all around the place. But, yes, every elephant tends to get lazy and fat if they are successful, and they need a little flea on top of them. The best elephants are actually collections of fleas, collections of little small organisations. The best elephants are going 'globular', if I can mix all my metaphors, and turning themselves into groups of projects, in which everybody has quite a lot of room and space to use their initiative. If you peer inside some of the best elephants, they are actually made up of lots of little businesses.

John Quinn
Are there not people who will never make good fleas and work best in the elephants?

Charles Handy
Yes and it is terribly important. I always say that a new

organisation is a bit like a theatre company. The intellectual property, as it were, that distinguished people that you see in front of you, and the big names in the programme, are fleas, they come in from outside for the project. But the small names are the very important ones. They are the manager of the theatre, the front of house, the stage manager, the lighting people, they are there all the time to provide the infrastructure for the fleas and they are important. We need the elephants. At my publishers, all the people who write the books are outside, but all the people inside, the editors, the publicity people and so on, are important because they are the infrastructure. Fleas ride on the backs of elephants. My worry is that the elephants will be left with the second-best people, and not the best.

John Quinn
What is the connection between the threat to elephants and the rise in anti-globalisation?

Charles Handy
I think people are worried about the spill-over from capitalism and they are right to be worried. They are wrong to try and stop it in its tracks because capitalism is the only thing that lifts people out of poverty. If you stop capitalism, if you stop the market forces in society, people producing things and making money, nobody is going to get richer. One of the reasons Ireland, for all its problems, is a much better place than it was forty years ago, is because of capitalism, so let's not decry it too much. Isn't it an ironic thing that people who protest against globalisation do it with the Internet, with mobile phones, with aeroplanes, with all the things that capitalisation and globalisation has brought us.

John Quinn
What role can religion/spirituality play in the vacuum that exists? Is there a God? Come on, Charles, tell us!

Charles Handy
I can only talk personally here, can't I? I am always searching for
a deeper meaning in things. I believe that there is in all of us a
deeper truth and Marsilio Ficino is my philosopher of choice.
He was the philosopher for the Renaissance and a tutor to the
Medicis and he said that the point of life was to bring your soul
to light, and by the soul he meant that which is potentially
greatest within you. I believe that the spiritual life, the
reflective, meditative life, is about getting in touch with your
soul, that we then need to go out and do something and bring
our soul to light, to put what is potentially the greatest within
you to some use.

WORKING WITH CHANGE

Anne Coughlan

I am here today to talk about work-life balance issues from an employer or business perspective. I have worked for the Irish Business and Employers Confederation (IBEC) for almost twenty years as a researcher. For those of you who are unaware of IBEC, it is a non-profit making employer organisation, representing the interests of around 7,000 businesses and organisations in Ireland. Its function is to represent business needs at local, national and international levels. It provides a variety of services to its member companies, such as representation at negotiations, information and training, legal advice, and so on. More recently IBEC has been responsible for implementing a number of family-friendly/work-life balance programmes within IBEC and for member companies. Before talking about these programmes and looking at some of the reasons why IBEC is involved in this area, I would like to take a few moments to tell you about my own experience, which has led me to work in this area.

A number of years ago, I had made a decision to return to college to undertake a masters degree by research thesis. I had been thinking about this for some time but found it difficult to decide on a topic. During my time with IBEC I had seen many changes in both the role of business in the Irish economy and in the focus of work in IBEC. One of the main changes that I had seen was that while union/management relationships were still very high on the agenda within IBEC, there was a shift in concern towards the social and personal within employment. Much of the management literature was concentrating on issues related to employee development and motivation. Any of you here who are working in, or have taken any courses in, human resources, will be very familiar with concepts like employee involvement, reward payment schemes, communications, performance appraisal, team working and training. A growing body of evidence began to build up showing that the long term success of any organisation depended to a large extent on its people, i.e. their level of commitment, expertise, creativity and dedication to quality and customer care. Good people management could lead to direct bottom line benefits in terms of overall business performance.

With the development of the Irish economy, the role of human resources in organisations shifted somewhat away from issues of re-structuring, down-sizing and redundancies, towards how to realise the potential of employees. Having 'your employees with you' and developing their unique potential, meant that the organisation stood a better chance in a globally competitive environment – in other words, employees could help companies gain a competitive edge.

As a result of these developments, I decided to focus on employee values for my research thesis. I wanted to explore what employees valued most in terms of being at work. Six months into my study I changed my subject to flexible working. The major trends that emerged from my research and observation was an increasing tendency for people to struggle with lives that required 'juggling'. Someone coined the phrase 'the sandwich generation' to describe what it felt like for working parents to have children to look after on one side and elderly parents on the other. People were juggling their lives – think what that means for a moment. A juggler has a number of objects in the air, constantly moving. He or she cannot take their eye of the objects for even one second. It is an exciting activity initially – *look what I can do* – but then you start to wonder when you can stop. The objects in the air for most people include work, children, relationships, elderly parents, time for oneself, the traffic, paying mortgages, to name but some. Quality of life – a popular phrase in recent years – was, for many, an abstract concept.

To return to the main part of my presentation, I am here today to talk about business and work-life balance. I will do this, firstly, by putting the issue in the broader context of the Irish economy and social partnership. Secondly, I will examine what exactly work-life balance is and whether it has actually caught on in Irish business. Thirdly, I will spend a little time speculating about the workplace of the future and finally, I will address the question of the conference: Is the future my responsibility?

Back in 1988 when the first of the recent National Pay Agreements, the Programme for National Recovery (PNR), was negotiated, the economic outlook for Ireland was grim. The public finances were out of control. The numbers in employment had been reducing for a number of years and large-scale emigration had once again become a feature of Irish life. We all remember when the figures for unemployment started to go over the quarter of a million and how stubbornly high they remained for a long time.

From Table 1 (overleaf) you can see that in the thirteen-year period between 1988 and 2001 our population grew by around 300,000, the numbers in employment grew by more than half a million and the numbers on the live register went down by

1: Key Changes 1988 - 2001

	1988	2001	% Change
Population	3.5m	3.8m	+7.3%
Employment	1.1m	1.7m	+50%
Unemployment	217,000	75,000	-65%
GNP Per Head	£5,680	£15,773	+178%

Source: Dept. of Finance Budgetary and Economic Statistics – March 2001

142,000. GNP, a measure of living standards per head of population, almost trebled in absolute terms during this period, or doubled when inflation is taken into account.

There is a general agreement that the partnership approach in the national agreements played a crucial role in aiding the recovery and successful development of the economy over the last decade and a half. One of the major themes that has emerged over the years from the various national agreements negotiated by the social partners has been the importance of an inclusive social policy agenda. In the last agreement, the Programme for Prosperity and Fairness, the social partners made commitments to the programmes and employment initiatives including equality, childcare, disability, the elderly and racism. Also under this agreement, a committee was established with the task of developing and implementing a national framework for the development of family-friendly policies at the level of the enterprise. The committee, now in operation for over a year, is made up of employer, trade union and government department representatives and the Equality Authority. (See Table 2)

2: Objectives of National Framework Committee

- Develop policies at the level of the enterprise
- Develop practical guidelines
- Disseminate Information
- Identify best practice
- Identify potential barriers and impediments
- Monitor and report on developments
- Provide training to management, unions, employers and workplace representatives

To date the National Framework Committee has achieved the following objectives:

- Family-friendly Website
- National Workplace Family-Friendly Day – 1st March
- Newsletter
- Regional Information Seminars
- Approval of Funding Proposals
- Commissioning of Benchmarking Study

So why are we talking about family-friendly work-life balance issues now? What are the main drivers for change?

- *Skill & Labour Shortages* – Initially, employers became interested in family-friendly/work-life balance policies as a response to skill shortages. Back in 1999, labour force projections indicated that the natural increase in the population over the next few years, would only be capable of supplying approximately half of the demand for labour. Debates on how to increase the labour supply focused on increasing participation rates for women, as well as moving people from being unemployed to employed and relying on net immigration. Irish women's participation in the labour market has advanced swiftly over the previous 20 years. Just over a third of working age women were active in the labour market in 1983. By 1998, more than half of all Irish women of working age were in the labour force. Between 1991 and 1999 women had filled three out of every five jobs added to the national workforce. Women were projected to contribute 58 per cent of the increase in the labour force in the years to 2011 (Medium Term Labour Market Review, 2000, FÁS). However, there were still a number of issues blocking women's retention and re-entry to the labour force. These barriers included the tax system, the high cost and lack of suitable childcare, lack of appropriate skills and unsuitable hours of work. One of the ways suggested for addressing some of these difficulties was through the provision of family-friendly/work-life balance policies.

- *Demographics* were a second major force for change. While the birth rate in Europe fell rapidly after the post-war baby boom, it continued at a high level in Ireland until 1980, after which time it declined. The total fertility rate at over 1.9 in Ireland is currently well over that in other EU countries, but it is expected to fall towards the EU average of 1.4. Alongside the rest of the world, we will see a rapid growth of the older population and the shrinking of the younger generation. In effect what this means is that we are not and will not be reproducing ourselves. There is a real concern as to where our future workforce will come from.

- *Stress and Quality of Life Issues* – The problems employees are having coping with the work and non-work areas of their lives are described above.

- *Demand from Trade Union Members and Employees* – The difficulties employees are experiencing have been reflected both in the Irish Congress of Trade Unions's survey of members which showed that family-friendly issues were the next most important issue after pay, and in IBEC's most recent Annual National Survey on Pay and Conditions of Employment in the Manufacturing sector (2001), where around four out of ten companies reported increased demand from staff for flexible working arrangements.

- *Culture Change* – Another element of change has been our culture. Research in the UK and the US has shown that young people do not want to work in the same way as their parents did. Many had seen their parents spend most of their lives working for little personal benefit. Many of you must have a relation who has been among one of the young people who are spending a year in Australia. Other cultural changes include the fact that women want to work outside the home. Many have a third level qualification – in fact, in 1996, more than half (51 per cent) of all third level students were female. The 'breadwinner' model, where the male went into paid employment and the women stayed at home and minded the family, no longer works for many people. Many women with children have no choice but to work. Married women's participation in the labour force increased eight-fold over the last 30 years from around 38,000 in 1971 to 330,000 in 2001. Men too wanted time to be more involved with their families. The long-hours work culture in many organisations did not facilitate this.

So what are family-friendly/work-life balance policies? There is nothing earth-shattering about what makes up these policies, but their impact can be far reaching. A quick word on the difference between the terms 'family-friendly' and 'work-life balance'. Family-friendly policies tend to be focused on the needs of working mothers, while work-life strategies embrace the needs of different people at different stages of their life. It is often set within a broader diversity strategy, which recognises the needs of different groups of workers. The issue of work-life balance came about as organisations began to look at supporting the needs of all their employees and not only working mothers with young children. It encompasses the notion of differences being valued and understood. It also holds that individuals at all stages of their lives work best when they are able to achieve an appropriate balance between work and all other aspects of their lives. I am using the two terms interchangeable here because 'family-friendly' are the words used in the PPF, to which IBEC and ICTU made a commitment. We have found however, that most companies and employees prefer the term 'work-life balance'.

Family-friendly work-life balance policies include *flexible working arrangements*, i.e. flexibility with regard to the time and place of work, such as part-time work, job sharing, teleworking/home-working, flexitime, compressed working week, and annual hours. Other possible policies include flexible leave arrangements, voluntary breaks, childcare support, resources and referral services, employee assistance programmes, and work-life balance training for managers. Many organisations already have these policies, mainly on an informal basis.

But what is in it for business in addition to addressing skill and labour shortages? The principal arguments are that such policies reduce casual sickness absences/lateness, improve recruitment/retention, improve motivation/morale/commitment, provide cost savings, reduce stress levels, and enhance corporate image.

In relation to the business arguments there are many in addition to that of skill shortages:

- Employees will not have to use company time to deal with family-related issues.
- Female employees will return after maternity leave.
- 'Happy staff make happy customers'. In a study carried out by the Industrial Society in the UK (called 'Time Out') it was

shown that those with autonomy over their working time were happier in their jobs. The knock-on effects of this is higher staff morale and better customer relations.

- Family-friendly policies are an important way to enhance the organisation's reputation with customers and in the community.
- A company can become an 'Employer of Choice', i.e. your company will be recognised in a competitive labour market as being a good place to work.
- Failure to address emerging work-life issues may impact negatively on the business in terms of reducing both employee productivity and customer satisfaction.

Incidence & Take-Up

The next two tables provide some information on the incidence and take-up of flexible working arrangements in Ireland.

3: Incidence of Flexible Working Arrangements – IBEC Surveys

- Manufacturing and Wholesale Dist. – 2001   73%
- Financial Services Sector – 2001   64%
- Retail Sector – 2001   73%

Four out of ten companies in this survey experienced increased demand from employees for flexible working arrangements, while a third of the companies had increased their usage of flexible working arrangements over the previous twelve months.

The State too has been active in this area, both as a policy maker and as an employer. To date, in terms of leave arrangements, the State has introduced Carers Leave, Parental Leave and Force Majeure. It has also extended Maternity and Adoptive Leave. Its policy in relation to childcare has in the main been about funding the expansion of the supply of childcare through capital grants and increasing the level of Child Benefit, payable to all parents. The State as a large employer has introduced a number of flexible working arrangements, such as job-sharing and career breaks. More recently, it brought in term-time working and work-sharing.

With regard to the private sector, while many organisations indicated that they provide some form of flexibility, the take up is somewhat low, with the exception of part-time work.

4: Percentage of Employees on Some Form of Flexible Working Arrangement

- IBEC Study of Mfr and W/sale Dist. – 2001   10%

- Quarterly National Household Survey
  – 1st Quarter – 2001 (part-time only)   17%

- IBEC Survey in the Financial Services Sector
  – 2001   19%

- IBEC Survey in the Retail Sector – 2001   27%

The UK, which also has a national programme on work-life balance led by the Blair Government, started looking at these issues many years ago. More wide-scale research has been carried out there on many issues related to work-life balance. I would like to draw your attention to two pieces of research briefly. The first, called *Work-Life Balance 2000: Baseline Study of work-life balance practices in Great Britain*,[1] surveyed 2,500 workplaces and 7,500 employees. Some of the main findings mirrored those of Ireland and were:

- Around 6 out of 10 workplaces had some form of flexibility.
- Other than part-time work only a small proportion of workers practiced flexible working arrangements.

- There was a substantial demand from employees for flexible working arrangements.

Other findings indicated that

- There was a high level of support from both employers and employees for work-life balance.
- One in five employees worked from home at least some of the time – predominantly managers and professional workers and more males than females. A third of employees not working from home said they would like to.
- The majority of women returning from maternity leave switched to part-time work.
- More women preferred greater flexibility in their working arrangements on their return to work than longer maternity leave.
- Employers were more concerned about the potential unfairness arising out of work-life balance practices than employees were.

Lest you think that work-life balance is still only about women and children, the second piece of research that I would like to refer to is *Work Life Balance – Survey of 6,000 UK Managers, Senior Managers & Directors 1998.*[2]

- Over half (53 per cent) of the respondents spend between 41-50 hours at work and a further 26 per cent spend more than 51 hours in an average week.
- Over half of the respondents (55 per cent) would choose to work longer hours over a four day week.
- Around 40 per cent of those surveyed would prefer an earlier start, with an earlier finishing time. Around a quarter would prefer some form of flexible working arrangement with regard to start and finish times. There was little enthusiasm for working late.

- Around a quarter would trade lower pay in exchange for more personal time.
- Close to half of the respondents were finding it increasingly difficult to meet both personal and work commitments.
- Two-thirds say that working long hours is confused with commitment and around four in ten of those responding felt that within their organisation working long hours has more to do with inefficiency than with the workload involved.
- Over eight out of ten respondents felt that they had sacrificed something important at home for the sake of their career – the two largest sacrifices being 'missing children growing up' and 'putting work before family'.
- In terms of what changes respondents would like to make in order to improve their work-life balance, the top priority was to work fewer hours followed by a desire to change the culture of the organisation for which they work.

I will return to the question later of why – given that there is such a need and demand for flexible working arrangements – the take-up is so low.

There are, however, a number of difficulties to overcome, both for managers who wish to implement family-friendly/work-life balance policies and for employees who may wish to avail of them. For the former group, there is the difficulty of convincing senior management of the business arguments for such policies. While there is often support for these issues from the human resources/personnel department, the overall business of the organisation may be running to a different agenda. There is also the issue of the 'long hours culture' and how family-friendly/work-life balance policies fits with this. Employers are often afraid that if they provide flexible options for staff, that all staff will want them. They are also concerned about the costs and legal implications of having such arrangements, as well as fairness (i.e. is it fair on other full-time staff?) and trust issues (how do you manage staff who work from home?).

Employees on the other hand, are wary about loss of status and the impact on their career if they avail of these arrangements. They are also concerned about their relationships with colleagues and potential resentments. Employees too are fearful of change, and while believing that such arrangements are a good idea, do not think that they would work for them. In some organisations also, flexible working arrangements are not an available option for staff.

The Workplace Of The Future

Can we predict the future? Could we have predicted ten years ago an Ireland with almost full-employment? Did we even think last Christmas that we would be talking about a recession as soon as this? Back in the 1960s we imagined that we would be a leisure society by now. Many envisioned the flowering of capitalism not as more work, but as increasing leisure. So what happened? According to one commentator (Benjamin K Hunnicutt[3]), there are a number of reasons why the leisure society has not happened.

1. *Consumerism* – people have chosen luxury instead of leisure. In a paradoxical way, people spend more money on luxuries to compensate for lack of time and at the same time have to earn more money and work harder to pay for the luxuries.

2. *Politics* – Governments (until recently) have positioned themselves as the guardians of full-time work – jobs are the ultimate ideal. Full employment is the great societal goal.

3. *Cultural Shift* – work has become the new religion in the developed world. People get their sense of identity and purpose in life from their work. Work has become an end in

itself, as opposed to a means to an end. Pursuing leisure or other such-like activities is viewed as trivial.

According to ESRI's latest Medium Term Review (Sept 2001), as Ireland is now one of the richest countries in the world, the choices made by individuals about how best to improve their well-being may be rather different than in the past. The standard of living in the US, measured in terms of GDP per head, is considerable higher than in the EU. However, when output per hour is looked at, there is a smaller gap. What this means is that the difference in 'living standards' between the EU and the US is due to a preference among the population of the EU for more leisure at the expense of less money income, or a 'higher leisure substitution effect' as economists term it.

In Ireland, while we do take longer holidays than the US, hours of work in manufacturing remain longer than the average in the EU, though less than in the US. Over the coming decade, according to the ESRI, the Irish labour force will have a choice between maintaining hours worked or taking the potential rise in income as more leisure. They argue, therefore, for greater flexibility in the labour market to accommodate individuals' different preferences – where some choose an increase in money income and others choose a smaller increase combined with more leisure. Employees may choose family-friendly/work-life balance policies at the expense of some reduction in measured income.

Given the present uncertainty in the Irish economy, it may seem unwise to attempt to predict what way employee expectations may go in the future. Bearing this in mind, however, it is fair to say that employees will not necessarily expect to be doing the same job all their lives. In the modern economy, with many high-tech firms, companies may grow and contract more frequently and employees may face more frequent changes in employment. With this frequent mobility employees will expect flexible contracts and reward packages.

Employees will want to work for a company brand they respect and will expect the organisation to recognise diversity, i.e. to recognise the value of difference in the workplace. Knowledge will be the key resource in what will be the next society, according to Peter Drucker.[4] (Knowledge workers, or people whose jobs require formal and advanced schooling, now account for a third of the American workforce, outnumbering factory workers two to one.) Knowledge workers see themselves as equal to the organisations that employ them – they see themselves as professionals rather than 'employees'.

Is the Future my Responsibility?

In the 1980s many had the attitude that greed was good. What Adam Smith actually said was that the pursuit of personal interest can be transformed into the common good. It is the coming together of mutual interests of business and society that can potentially lead to the common good. Society needs business to create wealth – to take risks, to invest and to speculate. But it is the responsibility of society to balance out the wealth created and to create an inclusive social agenda. In a capitalist society, the primary responsibility of business is to its shareholders. Its role is to create wealth. Other responsibilities come from that, such as the responsibility to be a fair and just employer and to act responsibly in relation to the community and the environment. The extent of the profit, what it means to be a just and fair employer and what responsibility they should have in relation to the environment, can and is determined by others. In a world where the continued existence of a business is linked to its ability to provide shareholders with the best return on their investment in a highly competitive environment, business is not going to like or want restrictions on its capacity to create profit. Governments in their deliberations, particularly in relation to taxation policy, have to struggle with the balancing of the business alongside the social agenda.

IBEC considers it's responsibility now and in the future
- to provide employers with the information they need to do their jobs;
- to lobby and represent business interests at national, EU and international level;
- to promote best practice across a range of employment issues for employers in this country.

The employee agenda in this country has primarily been driven by legislation, often emanating from the EU. However, much of the recent employment-related social policy has emerged from the partnership agreements negotiated by the social partners. While the initial focus of the partnership agreements was on purely economic issues, the increasing inclusion of social policy issues is an acknowledgement by business of the importance of this area, both to business and to society in general. The Framework Agreement on Family-friendly Policies at the Level of the Enterprise is an example of a partnership solution to a societal and business issue

In addition to our participation on the National Framework Committee and as part of our commitment to move this agenda forward, IBEC is implementing a number of initiatives including the provision of information, advice and training on family/work–life balance issues. Through these initiatives, IBEC, along with both ICTU and Government Departments, hope to encourage and support the development of family-friendly and balanced workplaces in every practical way.

Notes

1. Carried out by The Institute for Employment Research at the University of Warwick and IFF Research, an independent market research agency.
2. *The Great Work/Life Debate – The Definitive Report*, WFD/Management Today, 1998.
3. 'The Historical Origins of the Time Famine' – A Paper presented

at the APA/NIOH Interdisciplinary Conference on Work, Stress and Health in Baltimore, March 11-13, 1999, during the Symposium on OVERWORK: CAUSES AND CONSEQUENCES, by Benjamin Kline Hunnicutt, Professor, The University of Iowa.

4.   'The Next Society', *The Economist*, Nov. 3rd 2001.

CIVIC EXPRESSION
THE VALUE OF VOLUNTEERING

Freda Donoghue

Introduction

In response to the UN International Year of the Volunteer in 2001, the Irish Government established the National Committee on Volunteering, set up under both the *Programme for Prosperity and Fairness* and the White Paper, *Supporting Voluntary Activity*. The NCV will sit until the end of 2002, that is, one year after the end of the International Year of the Volunteer. The White Paper also advised the establishment of an Implementation and Advisory Group, which was convened over the summer of 2001, and which will meet regularly in order to implement various aspects of the White Paper. Clearly, therefore, there is policy-level interest in the voluntary and community sector and, for many involved in the sector, whether as practitioners or observers, there is a sense that finally things are beginning to happen. In addition, the place of the Community and Voluntary Pillar at the national policy-making table – at the negotiations for national programmes of government for example – are another sign of the growing public face of volunteering.

At the same time, there is a growing body of research on the sector and a small but growing research community interested in the policy, practice and enquiry nexus. This community has helped to inform practitioners and policy makers of important and current developments and this paper will present some of those findings. Coming from a perspective of the importance of the sector, and of volunteers, this paper will examine data on the sector's economic value and the economic value of volunteers. The paper will argue, however, that volunteers, and the voluntary sector, are more important than purely operating with an economic paradigm would suggest. Developing that theme, the paper will examine, in some depth, volunteering in Ireland, using the most available data. Incorporating the current debate on social capital, the paper argues for the importance of placing the 'self' in any discussion on volunteering.

Indeed, as will be seen, volunteering must be examined allowing for the perspective of the individual, the voluntary organisation and wider society to be included. Voluntary organisations do more than provide services. They are about citizenship, community belonging and civic expression. They are one way in which social cohesion is generated and are important building blocks in societal sustainability. Yet, as will be seen later, volunteering, which is about the expression of the civic self, may only be occurring among certain social groups. This raises challenges for organisations and for society, challenges that will need to be addressed in order to enhance the greater social and civic value of volunteering.

The Nonprofit or Voluntary Sector in Ireland

Data from 1995 show the economic contribution of the nonprofit or voluntary sector in Ireland. The nonprofit sector comprises organisations as diverse as voluntary hospitals, voluntary schools, sports organisations, arts and cultural organisations, community development associations, organisations dealing with social services, environmental organisations, lesbian and gay organisations, tenants' rights, travellers' rights, rural development organisations and housing associations. In Ireland these organisations spent a total of €4.2bn in cash terms. When compared as a proportion of GDP or GNP for that year, the Irish nonprofit sector was worth 8.6 per cent of GDP and 9.5 per cent of GNP.[1]

Indeed, the nonprofit sector in 1995 was worth more – in its expenditure – than agriculture and fishing, which spent €3.62bn and almost twice as much as public administration and defence, which spent €2.22bn. To adopt an economic paradigm for the sector might seem a little unusual in an Irish context. The sector in Ireland is never generally thought of in economic terms, perhaps because of what has been described as the myth of 'goodness' associated with the sector.[2] The association of the sector with doing good can mean that the sector's importance is only perceived as occurring at a level on a par with saintliness, and therefore unmeasurable. An economic lens, however, places the focus firmly on what the economy benefits from such activities and can start to open up the question of the greater importance of the sector. Of course, the myth of goodness begs several questions, one of which is whether 'goodness' itself has a price or is worth something economically. It must also be asked whether the sector really is about goodness and what has the effect of that myth been on the perceived effectiveness of the sector.

While these are interesting questions, and worth keeping in mind, I wish to explore one aspect of, or contributor to that supposed goodness, namely the volunteer. Indeed, the volunteer can be seen in some ways as the very repository of such goodness. If the nonprofit sector is about goodness, those who are perceived to be the heart of such goodness are volunteers, the unpaid labourers of the voluntary sector (and I use the term 'unpaid labourer' advisedly here).

The Value of Volunteering

Without yet abandoning the economic argument, I would first like to examine the cash value of the volunteer. What is the unpaid labour of volunteers worth and how do these unpaid labourers compare with their paid counterparts in the Irish nonprofit sector? In 1995, it was calculated that volunteers were worth €598m to the Irish economy. Their contribution increased the sectors value from €4.2bn to almost €4.8bn, or 11 per cent of GNP.[3]

The contribution of volunteers can also be seen in another way. In 1995 there were 125,584 (full-time equivalent or FTE) paid employees in the Irish nonprofit sector. As a proportion of the non-agricultural labour force, they were equal to 12 per cent. The addition of 33,690 (FTE) volunteers increased that contribution to the labour force to 15 per cent. With the inclusion of volunteers, therefore, there were 159,274 (FTE) employees in the nonprofit sector. Volunteers comprised one fifth (21%) of all workers in the sector and were, themselves, equivalent to 27 per cent of the paid nonprofit sector workforce. Table One (overleaf) gives some indication of the 'might' of the sector, resident in its labour force, both paid and unpaid.

Clearly, therefore, volunteers are a significant force and one which, apart from being a key defining characteristic of the sector, are also critical to its operations, existence and future survival.[4]

The Voluntary and Community Sector in Ireland

Before moving on to examining volunteering in Ireland in more detail, I would first like to cast an eye over the voluntary and community sector. As noted above, the sector in Ireland is usually called the voluntary and community sector. While its exact components have never been clearly defined, it is usually taken to exclude voluntary secondary schools and third-level educational establishments, all of which satisfy the Structural-

Table One: Employment in Ireland by Industry 1995 (FTE)*

Industry	No. (FTE 000)
Manufacturing	247.5
Agriculture, Forestry and Fishing	210.2
Professional Services	192.6
Nonprofit Sector (paid and volunteer employment)	159.3
Retail Distribution	147.9
Nonprofit Sector (paid employment only)	125.6
Personal Services	83.7
Building and Construction	82.8
Insurance, Financial and Business Services	77.6
Transport, Communications and Storage	77.5
Wholesale Distribution	46.9
Public Administration and Defence	34.9
Other Industrial (not elsewhere stated)	26.0
Electricity, Gas and Water	13.2
Mining Quarrying and Turf	5.6

*FTE was calculated by applying a ratio based on the average number of hours worked in one week for each sector compared with the average number of hours per week for the total labour force. The original data were obtained from Central Statistics Office (1996).

Operational definition, have charitable purposes and hold charity numbers. The position of voluntary hospitals within the parameters of the voluntary and community sector is less clear but for the purposes of this paper I will exclude them, not because they are not part of the voluntary picture but because I wish to look at data that are not too biased in favour of large institutions in receipt of significant government funding. By so doing, I hope to emphasise the input of volunteers and their importance, for they are clearly more important to some parts of the sector than to others.

Focusing on this smaller voluntary and community sector, therefore, there were 32,136 FTE paid employees. This proportion was almost matched by the number of volunteers at 31,919. In other words, 49 per cent of all employment in the voluntary and community sector was composed of volunteers. Table Two gives a breakdown of employment in the voluntary and community sector in 1995.

Table Two:
Employment in the Voluntary and Community Sector 1995

	Paid Employees (%)	Volunteers (%)	Paid Employees & Volunteers (%)
Social Services	16.6	44.7	30.6
Culture and Recreation	22.3	27.0	24.6
Religion	21.5	6.4	14.0
Development & Housing	15.8	10.8	13.3
Health	10.0	4.3	7.1
Education & Research	7.5	0.3	3.9
Environment	3.3	0.7	2.0
Foundations	0.4	2.8	1.6
Civic and Advocacy	1.4	0.7	0.9
Not Elsewhere Classified		1.6	0.7
Total (N)	32,136	31,919	64,055

These data show that the power of the voluntary and community sector lies in its employees. Just over three per cent of the non-agricultural labour force is in paid employment in the voluntary and community sector but this proportion almost doubles, to six per cent, when voluntary labour is included. The powerhouse of the sector, therefore, is in all of its employees, the tasks that these workers perform for the organisations, the responsibilities and the roles that they hold. As we will see, shortly, it is also about their value, not only their economic value but their wider value.

Expenditure of this sector amounted to €1,066m. This means that in 1995, the voluntary and community sector contributed half as much as public administration and defence to the economy. Furthermore, when an imputed value was placed on the labour of volunteers and allowed as an in-kind expenditure, the expenditure of the sector came to €1.61bn. This contribution was worth three-quarters that of public administration and almost half the contribution made by agriculture, forestry and fishing.

A Greater Value?
There is more to the picture of volunteering, therefore, than can be captured through an economic lens, and as already suggested, the tendency in Ireland is take a non-fiscal view of this activity. Before leaving the economic argument to one side, however, it is worth keeping in mind, in these days of cash awareness, that volunteers have a price and do make a small but important contribution to the Irish economy.

An economic focus, however, does not tell us anything about why volunteers get involved and what the 'meaning' of volunteering is. Indeed, economic explanations of volunteering have tended to be insufficient to explain the role of the individual in volunteering, that is, why an individual should engage in volunteering which is usually associated with altruism[5] or the myth of goodness. This paper will now examine some data on volunteering in Ireland to see if a value different from, and in addition to, the economic one can be deciphered and what this value comprises.

Volunteering has been defined in the recent White Paper, taking its cue from the Volunteer Resource Centre, as 'the commitment of time and energy, for the benefit of society, local communities, individuals outside the immediate family, the environment or other causes. Voluntary activities are undertaken of a person's own free will, without payment (except for reimbursement of out-of-pocket expenses)'.[6]

This definition is similar to that used in three nationwide studies conducted on volunteering in Ireland during the 1990s by the Policy Research Centre at the National College of Ireland. According to a study published in 1999, '[b]y voluntary work we mean any activity that is unpaid and is carried out by free choice for the benefit of people, other than or in addition to yourself or your own immediate family, or for the benefit of animals or the environment. These activities may be carried out through, or with, an organisation or group, church group, society or association, sports club, self-help group, voluntary group. Just being a member of an organisation or group doesn't count – what we're talking about here is the activity you carry out to help others for no monetary pay. These activities may also be carried out on your own and not arranged through an organisation of group.'[7] Volunteering, therefore, can take place within or outside of an organisation but is carried out for no monetary gain for the individual engaged in that activity. In other words, referring back to the myth about the sector's goodness noted above, the idea of volunteerism also connotes goodness, or benefit, and already, therefore, we can see how the meaning of volunteerism and the voluntary sector elide.

Definitions of volunteering, as can be seen, are based on the individual, and implicitly, on the individual motivation to become involved or engaged in some act of benefit outside the immediate self or family network.[8] Volunteering, therefore, involves the self engaged in what is generally perceived to be a selfless act, that is altruistic, but which is inherently about the self as the definition implies.[9]

Volunteers in Ireland

In the most recent survey on volunteering to date it was estimated that one third of all adults (aged over 18) were engaged in volunteering in Ireland.[10] Forty per cent of women volunteered compared with 28 per cent of men. In addition, volunteering rates had fallen over the 1990s from 39 per cent of the population in 1992 to 33 per cent in 1998.

As well as gender differences in the propensity to volunteer, there were also age differences. Those most likely to engage in volunteering were aged between 40 and 59, while those least likely to volunteer were aged over 60. Lower than average rates, but not significantly, were also to be found among those aged under 30. See Table Three.

Table Three: Volunteers by Age 1997-1998

Age Groups	%
18-29	31.1
30-39	32.8
40-49	40.8
50-59	47.8
60+	25.4
Total	33.3

Table Four presents data on the educational attainment of volunteers in the survey years 1997-1998. These data show that the tendency to volunteer rises with educational qualifications and above average volunteering rates are evident among those holding the Leaving Certificate, and, most particularly, those with a Third Level qualification.

Table Four: Educational Attainment of Volunteers 1997-1998

Education Level	%
Primary Certificate	23.2
Group/Intermediate Cert.	32.4
Leaving Certificate	39.2
Third Level Qualification	48.6
Total	33.3

Not surprisingly, given the link between educational attainment and volunteering, there is also a relationship between socio-economic status and voluntary activity. The tendency to volunteer is greater among the higher socio-economic groups, as shown in Table Five. Those respondents in unskilled manual jobs, or who were unemployed were among the least likely to participate in volunteering.

Table Five:
Socio-Economic Status of Volunteers in 1997-1998

Socio-Economic Group	%
AB (Professional and managerial)	44.3
C1 (Non-manual and administrative)	40.6
C2 (Skilled manual)	35.5
DE (Unskilled manual, unemployed)	25.9
F50+ (Farmers 50+ acres)	49.3
F50- (Farmers <50 acres)	10.7
Total	33.3

To briefly summarise the profile of volunteering presented so far, therefore, it appears that those who are aged in their middle years, have a higher educational qualification and higher socio-economic status are most likely to become volunteers. The challenge these data suggest is that there are certain social groups who are not participating as much as others and this may have important implications for social cohesion and social capital. Before engaging in that debate, however, I would now like to spend a few moments considering the motivations that volunteers report for volunteering.

Motivations for and Benefits of Involvement
Table Six presents the reasons given by volunteers in the 1997-1998 survey. As can be seen, belief in the cause was the

most important reason, followed by being asked to help, and with a fairly similar proportion of respondents, wanting to help.

Table Six: Reasons for Volunteering in 1997-1998*

Reasons	%
Belief in cause	42.9
Was asked to help	34.7
Wanted to help	32.1
Wanted to be neighbourly	29.8
Knew people involved	28.8
Time to spare	22.2
Enjoyment	19.6
Religious duty	12.8
Interest outside home	11.7

* Note that volunteers could choose more than one reason

Indeed, the motivations to volunteer, as can be seen in the table above, demonstrate a combination of different factors and individuals were allowed to name more than one reason in the survey. Some mix of idealism, altruism and pragmatism appears alongside a sense of enjoyment. What the data also indicate is the importance of engagement or participation. In other words, being part of a network or a community and thus being in a position to be 'asked to help', 'to be neighbourly', to 'want to help', or to already know 'those involved' are key to the expression of self in volunteering. Networks beget networks, participation leads to further participation, involvement aids social cohesion and the sustainability of society, or, at the micro level, social groupings, are implied by these data.

Indeed, the significance of belonging can be seen further if we examine the routes taken by volunteers to participating in voluntary activity.

As can be seen, in Table Seven, the routes to volunteering involving social networks are the most important for volunteers. The second most important was through an organisation, which also implies a sense of connectedness because volunteering was initiated in those instances either through membership of the organisation or through knowledge or awareness of the organisation's existence. It implies some sense of activity on the organisation's part – through holding meetings or distributing literature – but involves greater proaction on the part of the individual.

Table Seven: Routes to Volunteering in 1997-1998

Routes	%
Social networks	38.9
Organisational	30.1
Church or school	16.6
Mass media	3.5
Paid employment	3.5

Table Eight gives details of the main benefits cited by volunteers in 1997-1998. These findings are of interest because

Table Eight: Benefits of Volunteering in 1997-1998*

Benefits	%
Seeing results	54.1
Doing good	48.7
Meeting people	41.1
Enjoyment	34.4
Being appreciated	20.9
Gaining experience, skills	18.1
Forget own problems	17.3
Reward in heaven	13.8

* Note that volunteers could choose more than one benefit

they demonstrate a mix of functionalism (wanting to see something done), altruism (doing good) and socialising (meeting people). In addition, one third of volunteers cited the enjoyment factor of the activity.

The Non-Volunteer

In 1998, two thirds of the population did not engage in volunteering. It is of some use, therefore, to examine this population to see what their reasons were for not participating. As already noted above, non-volunteers were more likely to be male, older, or under 30, with lower educational attainment and in the lower socio-economic groups. Table Nine gives the main reasons cited by non-volunteers for not getting involved.

Table Nine: Reasons for Not Volunteering in 1997-1998*

Reasons	%
No time	51.9
Never thought about it	26.7
Was never asked	21.9
Too old	18.3
No transport	13.1
Did not think would like it	11.3

* Note that volunteers could choose more than one reason

Not surprisingly, and certainly a factor that has been noted by the media, not having enough time was cited by half of all non-volunteers in 1997-1998. Over a quarter of non-volunteers, however, said that they had never thought about volunteering, while over one fifth stated that they had never been asked.

If volunteering contributes to social capital[11] and is also a factor in social cohesion, there is a challenge for voluntary organisations to address these findings, namely that they must adopt creative ways for ensuring volunteering enters the public consciousness. It appears, too, that voluntary organisations need to be more proactive about asking for volunteers. It is to that wider discussion that my attention now turns.

The 'Meaning' of Volunteering

Voluntary activity is about society building and society sustaining. It involves the concept of commonality and community. It can also, as the history of the sector would show, imply a sense of Irishness (expressed for example through the GAA, Muintir na Tíre and the Catholic Church). Civic expression means the expression of the civic self, that is the self who is public, associated with the community, or at local level. The importance of the expression of the self or selves in society is about the individual – which volunteering is at some level – entering into relationships. The impetus to enter into such relationships may be idealism, the need to help, or may be relationally based or motivated. Even where individually based, the activity becomes relational, for where the impetus to become involved is belief in a cause, or the importance of an ideal, the result is finding expression with others who think or act similarly. This leads to the generation of social groups and social cohesion.

Voluntary activity is important as an expression of self, which I call the civic self here, only insofar as civic is about being a citizen. Indeed, this could be extended to include other kinds of 'selves' which may not necessarily be perceived as civic from the outside but which are about this expression (such as, for example, membership of the Taliban, IRA, freedom fighters). In other words, doing good does not necessarily have the monopoly on voluntary activity if doing good is only seen as the moral property of the dominant group in any one society. Doing good is not only relative but contextually bound and part of the meaning of volunteering where the notion of the public good, whoever that public is, is central. If, after all, voluntary means free will (and both German and Danish translations of volunteering are based explicitly on those two words), the notion of the individual or the self is inherent; not in an existentialist anomic fashion but as involving the social, civic actor. Indeed, it is interesting to relate the semiotics of the word volunteering with what we usually see as the essence of being human. In other words, we attribute our 'humanness' to having free will. Volunteering is one expression of that, and contains that explicitly in its lexicon.

Volunteering has a long history in Ireland.[12] Central to Irish peasant society was the practice of volunteering through *cooring* and the organisation of a *meitheal*. *Cooring* was essential to the maintenance of the social fabric of Irish peasant society up until the 1960s.[13] Volunteering was informal, to a large extent, but very much part of the social and society fabric, so in that sense there was some institutionalisation albeit through a process of enculturation. While volunteering has become more organisationally focused in more recent decades there are still some vital elements to consider. The association of volunteering with the concepts of 'charity' and with 'doing good' do not represent the full picture of volunteering in Ireland today. Indeed, just as in peasant days when there was an element of self interest (self sufficiency, self help) involved the self must always be remembered in this equation.

This expression of the self, the civic self, is an elemental part of volunteering. The involvement of the self whether for idealism, altruism or functional reasons leads to a relational engagement and thereby to the building of social units, social cohesion and societal sustainability. Volunteering, therefore, is important at the individual, organisational and societal levels. If, as the data suggest, certain groups are not participating, these groups are not benefiting from these 'ties that bind'. The range and spread of voluntary organisations (as shown earlier in the paper) indicate that voluntary activity is about more than service provision. Although there is a strong social service component to the voluntary sector in Ireland and service provision is the rationale for the provision of health board grants, such as Section 65 or Section 10 grants[14], volunteers are involved in many other activities. The contribution of volunteers to the fabric of society is about the construction of society. Fergus O'Ferrall has argued for the need for a philosophy of voluntary action in terms of the voluntary sector's position in Ireland.[15] As this paper suggests, there is also a need for a philosophy of volunteering. The relationship between the volunteer and society is not one-way. Not only does society, or the state, need volunteering, but the individual appears to need that activity too, as the motivations reported above indicate. The meaning of volunteering is more layered than either the 'doing good' or the service provision models would indicate. I hope that today I have started to reveal some of these layers in an effort to begin exploring that 'meaning'.

Notes

1. Freda Donoghue, Helmut K. Anheier and Lester M. Salamon, *Uncovering the Nonprofit Sector in Ireland: Its Economic Value and Significance*, 1999.

2. Gemma Donnelly-Cox and Gwen Jaffro, *The Voluntary Sector in the Republic of Ireland: Into the Twenty-First Century*, 1999.

3. This calculation was made by applying an average wage, supplied by the Central Statistics Office, to the hours put in by volunteers in a formal capacity, that is to an organisation. The Volunteer Resource Centre in Dublin has suggested that a similar calculation for volunteers involved in informal volunteering would almost double their imputed economic value.

4. As has been noted by voluntary organisations in the social service field, see Helen Ruddle and Freda Donoghue, *The Organisation of Volunteering*, 1995.

5. Andrew O'Regan, 'In Search of the Voluntary Sector: A Critical Review of the Literature', 1999.

6. Department of Social, Community and Family Affairs, 2000, p. 83.

7. Helen Ruddle and Ray Mulvihill, *Reaching Out: Charitable Giving and Volunteering in the Republic of Ireland, The 1997-8 Study*, 1999.

8. See Fred Powell and Donal Guerin, *Civil Society and Social Policy*, 1997.

9. See also O'Regan, op.cit.

10. Ruddle and Mulvihill, op.cit.

11. Freda Donoghue, 'Changing Patterns of Civic Engagement and Community Ties in Ireland', 2001.

12. J.J. Lee, 'History of the Irish Nonprofit Sector', forthcoming.

13. As detailed by Conrad M. Arensberg and Solon T. Kimball, *Family and Community in Ireland*, 1968; and Hugh Brody, *Inishkillane: Change and Decline in the West of Ireland*, 1973.

14. Section 65 grants are paid to health and social service organisations on the basis of their offering services that are 'similar or ancillary' to those provided by the State, from the original wording of the 1953 Health Act. Under the terms of 1991 Child Care Act, Section 10 grants were introduced for voluntary organisations in the field of child care and, again, the same wording was applied as a rationale for granting that funding.

15. Fergus O'Ferrall, *Citizenship and Public Service: Voluntary and Statutory Relationships in Irish Healthcare*, 2000.

References

Arensberg, Conrad M. and Kimball, Solon T., *Family and Community in Ireland*, Cambridge, Mass: Harvard University Press, 1968

Brody, Hugh, *Inishkillane: Change and Decline in the West of Ireland*, London: Allen Lane, 1973

Central Statistics Office, *Labour Force Survey 1995*, Dublin: Stationery Office, 1996

Department of Social, Community and Family Affairs, *Supporting Voluntary Activity: A White Paper on a Framework for Supporting Voluntary Activity and for Developing the Relationship between the State and the Community and Voluntary Sector*, Dublin: Stationery Office, 2000

Donnelly-Cox, Gemma and Jaffro, Gwen, *The Voluntary Sector in the Republic of Ireland: Into the Twenty-First Century*, Coleraine: Association for Voluntary Action Research in Ireland, 1999

Donoghue, Freda, 'Changing Patterns of Civic Engagement and Community Ties in Ireland', presented at *The Importance of Social Capital: International Lessons for Community Volunteering in Ireland*, organised by the Department of Social, Community and Family Affairs, Dublin, March, 2001

Donoghue, Freda, 'Defining the Nonprofit Sector: Ireland', *Working Papers of the Johns Hopkins Comparative Nonprofit Sector Project*, no. 28, edited by Lester M Salamon and Helmut K Anheier, Baltimore: The Johns Hopkins Institute for Policy Studies, 1998

Donoghue, Freda, *Reflecting the Relationships: An Exploration of the Relationships between the former Eastern Health Board and Voluntary Organisations in the Eastern Region*, Dublin: Eastern Regional Health Authority, forthcoming

Donoghue, Freda, Anheier, Helmut K., and Salamon, Lester M., *Uncovering the Nonprofit Sector in Ireland – Its Economic Value and Significance*, Dublin: The Johns Hopkins Institute for Policy Studies / National College of Ireland, 1999

Faughnan, Pauline and Kelleher, Patricia, *The Voluntary Sector and the State: A Study of Organisations in One Region*, Dublin: Conference of Major Religious Superiors, 1993

Lee, J.J., 'History of the Irish Nonprofit Sector' in Donoghue, Freda, *The Nonprofit Sector in Ireland*, forthcoming

O'Ferrall, Fergus, *Citizenship and Public Service: Voluntary and Statutory Relationships in Irish Healthcare*, Dublin: Adelaide Hospital Society, 2000

O'Regan, Andrew, 'In Search of the Voluntary Actor: A Critical Review of the Literature', paper presented at ARNOVA Conference, Washington DC, November, 1999

Powell, Fred and Guerin, Donal, *Civil Society and Social Policy*, Dublin: A&A Farmar, 1997

Ruddle, Helen and Mulvihill, Ray, *Reaching Out: Charitable Giving and Volunteering in the Republic of Ireland. The 1997-8 Survey*, Dublin: Policy Research Centre, National College of Ireland, 1999

Ruddle, Helen and Mulvihill, Ray, *Reaching Out: Charitable Giving and Volunteering in the Republic of Ireland – The 1994 Study*, Dublin: Policy Research Centre, National College of Industrial Relations, 1995

Ruddle, Helen and Donoghue, Freda, *The Organisation of Volunteering*, Dublin: Policy Research Centre, National College of Industrial Relations, 1995

Ruddle, Helen and O'Connor, Joyce, *Reaching Out: Charitable Giving and Volunteering in the Republic of Ireland*, Dublin: National College of Industrial Relations, 1993

Salamon, Lester M, Anheier, Helmut K., and Associates, *The Emerging Sector Revisited*, Baltimore: The Johns Hopkins Institute for Policy Studies, 1998

Salamon, Lester M and Anheier, Helmut K, *Defining the Nonprofit Sector. A Cross-National Analysis*, Manchester: Manchester University Press, 1997

IN EACH OTHER'S SHADOW[1]

Tom Healy

'Ar scáth a chéile a mhaireann na daoine'
'The people live in each other's shadow'

Where are we coming from?

The theme of this conference relates to the future. Preparing for the future is high on the agenda for individuals, communities and governments. As much as ever, uncertainty pervades our world and we need to review our current responses and institutional arrangements to meet future challenges. Yet, too often, there is a disconnection between the future and the present to the extent that the urgent drives out the important. What I would like to draw attention to in this contribution is the importance of:

- learning and community in meeting future and present challenges;
- the importance of a wider notion of well-being and the common good;

- the importance of 'joined-up' responses based on more reflection and strategic thinking.

I would like to support the claim that learning can provide the key to a successful reorientation and renewal of our societies that puts human well-being at the centre. However, learning is more than just what goes on in our individual worlds. We can and do learn as communities and organisations. We also learn from continually applying knowledge in new and old ways. 'Learning by doing' can add a new dimension to the important function of learning from the past. Perhaps we have conceived of a world in which the producers of knowledge and information in the media, universities and research laboratories have interpreted and analysed change. Then, as policy-makers and practitioners – whether in government, business or civil society – the rest of us have got on with living by devising the best solutions to meet the present, paying occasional regard to the findings of applied research and other sources.

Public policy makers tend, wisely, to stick with the fundamentals: providing the legal and security framework for property rights and the exercise of production, distribution and consumption. They help to provide the essential services, including some acceptable level of public education for most people, that would not otherwise be provided. More generally public authorities act to provide the right conditions and maintenance of civil order in which individuals and communities can realise their own good and that of each other.

We now have a stronger sense than ever before that some of the huge ideological experiments of the twentieth century ended where they ought to end. Can we conclude that the 'End of History' is as close as Francis Fukuyama and others would claim? Has liberal democracy triumphed once and for all? Perhaps the instinct for self-preservation and social co-operation is so firmly hard-wired into us through evolution or through cultural and spiritual influences that human civilisation can be spared and re-created in surprisingly new ways when all seemed lost or almost lost. On the other hand, the great visions of earthly utopia built around communism, liberalism, state welfare, capitalism, free trade and gobalisation have all failed in one way or another to fully resolve the quest at the centre of human existence. Charles Handy calls it the 'hungry spirit'. Whatever it is, the complications of being human imply ambiguity, freedom, conflict, uncertainty and a never-ending struggle to find the right answers in a world constantly torn between the forces of self-destruction and co-operation.

It has been remarked that the trouble with economics is that it is only 80 per cent correct. If each individual were only guided by pure calculating self-interest then at least some of human behaviour simply cannot be explained. We need to think on a wider plane. And yet, this is so difficult. It is not uncommon to encounter the view that fostering economic competitiveness should be the primary concern of the public policy. Or, the view that equality of opportunity should be the number one priority, or the environment or peace on this island or moral, civic or community renewal. The problem with single-track focus as well as single-track solutions is that they tend to ignore (i) the *complexity* of the world we live in, (ii) the *interdependence* and overlapping of environmental, economic, social spiritual and personal spaces and (iii) the *lack of consensus* on the kind of society or life we want.

Some things never change and one of these is the lament for loss of community and moral order. Writing in the nineteeth century, the French aristocrat, Alexis de Tocqueville, who travelled America and wrote extensively on the strength of civic norms there in contributing to democracy commented: 'Each [person] ... is a stranger to the fate of all the rest ... his children and his private friends constitute to him the whole of mankind; as for the rest of his fellow citizens, he is close to them but he sees them not ... he touches them but he feels them not; he exists but in himself and for himself alone.' More recently evidence has been produced by Professor Robert Putnam to show that social capital, which he defines to include networks and associated norms of reciprocity, is in the decline in the United States since the mid-1960s. His book, *Bowling Alone: the collapse and revival of American community*, has created a stir in senior policy circles in the US and beyond. The evidence from numerous sources suggests that people are voting less, joining less, volunteering less, giving less, trusting less and socialising less. Even the average annual number of family picnics is dramatically down over the last three decades!

Putnam does not ascribe these trends to economic factors alone such as increased working or commuting time or increases in economic inequality. His data point up a very strong *inter-generational* effect on social capital. Putnam advances the hypothesis that important historical conjunctures such as the so-called *Progressive Era* in the USA at the beginning of the twentieth century or the extraordinary civic zeal and national solidarity exhibited in the war effort in the 1940s left profound marks on the behaviour and preferences of whole generations at a crucial stage in history which persisted in the behaviour of the same generation over time.

The evidence for declining social capital is much less clear in Europe and other parts of the industrialised world. Evidence for a number of European countries as well as Australia and Japan, according to Putnam, point towards stability in many of the standard measures of social capital (notably levels and density of associational activity and informal sociability where data on the latter are readily available). However, one apparent exception is the level of inter-personal trust and especially trust towards institutions. Perhaps this is not surprising. The media leaves few stones unturned and whether or not institutions and governments are less trustworthy compared to the past, we are certainly much more aware of the existence and prevalence of corruption and other anti-social behaviour.

To date, evidence on trends and distribution of social capital in Ireland is incomplete and sketchy. The evidence on the larger context of institutional and value change is also difficult to interpret. Pending more evidence, I suggest that there are at least five reasons why we should not sit on the laurels of much deserved praise about our recent exceptional economic performance in Ireland:

- Increases in working time and greater intensity in work schedules, longer commuting time and perceptions of rising inequality may be endangering social capital – and this may be compounded by important culture shifts.
- There are grounds for thinking that the same processes observed in the USA may be at work elsewhere.
- The jury is still out on the likely long-term impact of new information and communication technologies
- There is a growing amount of suggestive evidence that the quality of social relations and ties do matter for all sorts of reasons.
- English-speaking countries frequently have more in common on a lot of political, social and labour market characteristics than other countries.

Finding the appropriate language and mental tools

The term human capital was coined in the early 1960s by economists to recognise the key importance of knowledge and skills in contributing to economic well-being. Human capital has been defined in a recent Organisation for Economic Co-operation and Development (OECD) report as 'The knowledge, skills, competencies and attributes embodied in individuals that facilitate the creation of personal, social and economics well being' (OECD, 2001, p. 18) This understanding of human capital emphasises the importance of a wide range of human capacities including non-cognitive skills and attributes as well as knowledge acquired through informal learning experiences.

Human capital and potential are the property of individuals. Social capital is the property of groups, communities and organisation. Many approaches to defining social capital are possible. The definition of social capital used in recent OECD report was: 'networks together with shared norms, values and understanding that facilitate co-operation within or among groups' (OECD, 2001, p. 41). This particular definition emphasises the role of shared norms and values as well as civic or social behaviour. Close to this understanding is the role of trust as a crucial mediating factor in assisting social co-operation whether at the level of an organisation, school or family.

One of the objections raised to the use of the term social capital is that its application does not distinguish between potentially destructive effects in some cases and types of networks on the one hand, and on the other, more positive ones providing a basis for greater social cohesion across diverse groups and cultures. We can all think of forms of social connectedness which are restrictive and possibly even highly destructive in certain circumstances. Some forms of social capital have the potential to bring social, personal and economic benefits not only to those directly engaged but also to others via spillover effects. Other forms or manifestations, particularly those that reside in tightly knit groups that exclude or mistrust outsiders, may serve to undermine broad social cohesion.

At last year's conference, 'Redefining Roles and Relationships', Professor Gearóid Ó Tuathaigh wisely cautioned us to 'watch our language'. Some may be uncomfortable with the language of 'capital' and may question its use in the context of resources or agents for the creation of human well-being. I will argue that there are at least three reasons why a judicious use of the term 'social capital' can be helpful:

1 it draws analytical attention to processes which are
   important and which frequently get sidelined because of
   the difficulty in observing, measuring and influencing
   them;
2 it provides a meeting place where different academic and
   research disciplines can start talking to each other and,
   more importantly;
3 it recognises the personal, social and economic benefits
   and costs of relating to others in a way that can help
   individuals, groups, communities and governments to
   invest more wisely.

My argument for defending the use of the term social capital
would repeat a defence of 'human capital'. Why should we
apply the notion of capital or resources only to tangible assets
such as buildings, machines and equipment? People, skills,
knowledge and values in communities, schools, families and
various organisations can also be crucial to the well-being of
nations. A tactical view on the use of language does not eschew
the spiritual, personal and cultural context or goals of learning
or social interaction, nor does it necessarily reduce social
relations and knowledge to some utilitarian good for the
achievement of some other end. Inter-personal relationships
and learning are their own reward.

What are we concerned about?
The starting point of the OECD report, *The Well-Being of Nations,
the role of human and social capital,* was consideration of a broad
range of economic, social and environmental concerns. As
citizens, we care about the cohesiveness of society and each
other's well-being. According to this way of thinking, an enlarged
notion of well-being can have at least four main dimensions:

• Sustainable consumption flows
• Sustainable capital stock – physical, natural, human and social

- Access to wealth, resources and income by different groups
- Subjective well-being and life satisfaction

A broad view of well-being, including economic well-being, goes beyond measures based on the market value of produced goods and services counted in the national accounts and subsumed in the well-known yardstick of progress – Gross National Product. Economic well-being includes the value of voluntary and unpaid labour, for example, as well as the effects of distribution of income and wealth. Certainly, Gross National Product is an important potential determinant and correlate of what one might call Gross National Happiness. But GNP does not equal GNH. GNP is a subset of economic well-being and economic well-being is a subset of total human well-being. A further consideration is that some activities or expenditures counted in GNP, although necessary, may not directly contribute to economic or total human well-being. Examples of what are termed 'social regrettables' include expenditure relating to pollution or various forms of social dysfunction including higher security or litigation costs associated with lower trust and anti-social behaviour.

Senior politicians are keenly aware of the international debate on social capital as evidenced by recent statements of both British and Irish Prime Ministers. At a conference on social capital held in Dublin in March 2001, the Taoiseach, Mr Bertie Ahern said:

I believe that social capital is a concept which deserves to be discussed in much greater depth. It has the potential to be a very positive influence in public policy development in this country and throughout the European Union. It is a concept which puts communities at the centre of our debates and it helps us to find a framework to explain and address the linkages between areas which are seemingly very different ... I would like today to mark the beginning of a much more

extensive consideration in this country of the many
complexities of the social capital concept. I believe that
academics, policy makers, professionals and the general
public would all benefit from a much deeper engagement in
the debate which you have been considering.

These views are also echoed in the remarks of the British Prime
Minister, Mr Tony Blair:

> The cutting edge work in social sciences is about the nature,
> limits and dynamics of co-operation, about trust and social
> capital, knowledge and human capital. The tide of debate
> has swung back to community, mutual responsibility and a
> cautious internationalism ('Third Way, phase two' *Prospect*,
> March, 2001).

A former Taoiseach, Mr John Bruton, said in December 1999:

> The enhancement of social capital in Ireland should be a key
> national objective and measure of success.
> If we try to measure social capital we will then be going
> some way towards devising a language of political
> discussion that will lead us to the right conclusions. So long
> as we continue on using the language of GDP, we will be
> drawn inexorably to the wrong conclusion.
> The work of volunteers is ignored in calculations of the
> Gross Domestic Product. The GDP only counts what is paid
> for in cash. The voluntary unpaid work of a parent caring
> for a child in the home is not counted in the GDP. Just being
> there to listen, to encourage – that is not counted in the
> GDP. The voluntary unpaid work of someone helping St
> Vincent De Paul is not counted in the GDP. Yet this work is,
> by any standard, part of the nation's social capital. Social
> capital is a network of relationship of trust, and of co-
> operation between people.[2]

The leader of the Labour Party, Mr Ruairí Quinn, stated at its recent annual party conference:

> We've had economic success over the last 10 years, but we've lost some things too. We work too hard and we sometimes have too little time for the important things in life. I can see some of you agreeing and we've lost a sense of collective spirit. But not completely. Congratulations are due to all directly involved in the battle against foot-and-mouth disease, including the Government. And our success proves a point. As a society we can work together cohesively. We can achieve. The community, properly motivated, remains a strong force in Irish society. But in recent years this strength hasn't been called upon or championed half enough. Too often greed and vested interests have replaced co-operation and compassion. Colleagues, it is time to build a new spirit of community ... for reasons that go beyond narrow or sectoral interests.

I have selectively quoted just a few expressions of political interest. Similar insights from other Irish political commentators could be cited. The key point and common thread underlying these expressions of interest in the community and social solidarity is that we need to think, plan and act on a broader plane than just the traditional measures of economic progress.

Happiness, Health, Learning and Wealth – taking the research evidence seriously

Work by economists such as Blanchflower, Oswald and Helliwell confirm the hypothesis that beyond a certain threshold, income matters less for life satisfaction than other factors. It appears that the quality of inter-personal relations and social ties together with important life events or experiences such as unemployment, education, divorce and health status become critical. At last years conference, Robert Lane described on-going research into the impact of a wide range of social and inter-personal factors on well-being or life satisfaction. The international research evidence reviewed in *The Well-Being of Nations* report also suggests diminishing returns to more income in terms of happiness or life satisfaction. Earn a certain level of income (if you are fortunate) and beyond that you get diminishing returns to more income but increased satisfaction from better health, education and especially better quality relations with others. '*Is fearr an tsláinte ná an t-ór*' (health is better than gold), an old saying in Irish, applies.

The relationship between social status and health is a common theme of research on population health.[3] This is founded on purchasing power (from income), knowledge power (from education) and employment power (from prestige and control). Alongside this more traditional approach, insights from psycho-social research have re-focused attention on the role of social ties and norms as important mediating factors in influencing the impact of income, education and employment on physical health and mental well-being. *The Well-Being of Nations* report suggests that the most convincing evidence of the likely positive impact of social ties lies in the area of personal health.

One of the key insights of the research reviewed by the OECD is that there is a strong potential link between human and social capital. Relationships of trust and reciprocal engagement presuppose particular skills and attributes of individuals. In the other direction, learning habits and effective learning and knowledge transfer presuppose a social setting in which people can learn in relationship with others. Arguably, we are innately both *learning* and *social* creatures by virtue of evolutionary hard wiring.[4] Evidence has already emerged from studies of the impact of home environment and school-related networks in providing support for better learning outcomes over and above the undeniable benefits of better teaching practice, school organisation and better focusing and targeting of physical and human resources within schools.

There are also likely to be significant impacts of social capital on economic well-being including growth in economic productivity. Early evidence on cross-country differences in GDP growth suggest a link between levels of trust and growth as well as between levels of trust and investment in physical capital. While much of the international evidence is still very tentative, there is enough to suggest that some of the recent Irish 'economic miracle' may be attributable to historical accumulations of values, norms and networks which facilitated entrepreneurship, lowered transactions costs and generally facilitated the impact of education, trade and investment on the domestic economy. Early evidence on cross-country differences in cross-country GDP growth over a 20 year period suggest a link between levels of trust and growth as well as between levels of trust and investment in physical capital.[5]

A call for more research or action or both?

Far from offering policy prescriptions, a renewed focus on social capital raises general policy design issues. *The Well-Being of Nations* report identifies a wide range of issues from flexibility in working time, education, transport and residential arrangements to the social position of families where public and private actors can leverage better quality social capital. However, social capital can never become the trojan horse to deliver economic and social progress. Many conditions and factors are required and no simple formula based on well identified policy levers is possible. Investing in social and human capital makes good sense for families, communities, business and government – if we can identify exactly what and how to invest time and money. Of course, not everyone has equal access to information, education, social networks or power. Calls for more lifelong learning, volunteering and civic responsibility are not enough. Giving poorer communities and disadvantaged groups a greater say and sense of responsibility is an important part of redressing social imbalance. In some cases, they may have the wrong kind of social capital or they may have plenty of social capital but not enough real access to financial or human capital to break out of cycles of poverty or exclusion.

Nostalgia for bygone social capital would be misplaced. Many of the important changes that have taken place in terms of changing labour market participation, greater equality of opportunity for men and women, greater emphasis on personal autonomy and self-expression, better health, more education and more consumer goods to enjoy are all very welcome. It is likely that social capital in Ireland, as elsewhere, is changing while newer and more welcome forms of association, involvement and civic engagement are emerging. There is no going back to the past and much of the social and economic under-development of the past is not a tribute to high social capital in Ireland, but rather a sign that the enormous potential and energy in individuals and communities were not fully realised or developed. The challenge is to reconcile what is positive in many of the new forms of association and participation in labour markets and society with a consideration for the wider needs of human well-being and justice. The ideological quarrels of another era and place should not deter efforts to identify the common ground and shared concern – which is much larger than might be apparent.

Re-thinking our values and assumptions

We may need to re-think the implicit assumptions, underlying values and patterns of public, private and voluntary provision appropriate to another phase in our development. We do need to acknowledge and enlarge concerns about measurable wealth and income to encompass quality of life and well-being – notoriously difficult as these are to account for. We – whether in private companies, public organisations or in civil society – also need to think through the implications of the way we live, work and learn on the strength of social ties and obligations. Getting the balance right calls for:

- farsightedness;
- 'joined-up' thinking;
- 'joined-up' action.

Farsightedness in most industrial democracies is difficult because it is easier to measure and deal with growth in income and productivity in this year's fiscal or electoral cycle. Yet, it has proved possible to put in place new and imaginative measures to provide for the future pension incomes of ageing populations.

'Joined-up' thinking based on an appreciation of interdependence is difficult because we are comfortable in our world, be it the discipline of economics, sociology or natural science or be it the Ministry of Finance or Transport or be it one sector or area of professional or industrial life. We know our objectives, we know our inputs and we do not want to muddy the picture.

'Joined-up' action is hard because it crosses public-private-voluntary efforts as well as research, policy and industrial or sectoral 'silo-pits' and calls for co-operation, trust and shared understandings and agendas. In a word, it calls for new types of social capital.

A long standing challenge in economic and social development is not only the creation of formal structures and institutions to facilitate co-operation and co-ordination, but also the creation and renewal of informal rules of behaviour, constraints, sanctions and internally imposed codes of conduct. Fostering an environment conducive to mutual help and care can provide a key link in the chain. Vital civic energy and social virtue can be released through more appropriate mechanisms and arrangements for mutual support.

A number of policy innovations based on small-scale projects using experimental research methods could yield useful information on community renewal and voluntary engagement. It is likely that 'top-down' or over-institutionalised solutions to encouraging voluntary effort and mutual community-based care will not be as effective as approaches which empower local communities to develop their own 'best practice'. An excessive reliance on 'top-down' approaches to levering social capital may rob it of its essential value as the property of spontaneous civil society working in partnership with public and corporate interests. In general, external or hierarchical control can crowd out intrinsic motivation to trust, engage or volunteer, especially where it does not acknowledge the capacities and trustworthiness of individuals (see Frey, 1999). Perhaps the greatest challenge to policy makers and others is how to bring about greater 'bridging social capital'. This is the type of social capital in which establishing links and reciprocal engagement across *different* groups is a key challenge in societies undergoing transition towards diversity, multi-ethnic diversity and pluralism in attitudes and expectations.

Passion, Vision and Virtue

Dr Maureen Gaffney, in her contribution to 'Redefining Roles and Relationships', spoke about rebuilding social capital in Ireland. She said: 'I believe that actions that are motivated by a deep purpose or basic value (for example, commitment to social justice) are imbued with a different kind of energy – more passionate, more altruistic, more capable of transcending the inevitable frustrations, more likely to end in coherent action'. In other words, I think that she is saying that we need more passion orientated towards the attainment of social equality and cohesion, or to use a more old-fashioned term, the common good. More of the following could be suggested:

- Passion and joined-up understandings and emotions being of one heart on the essentials;
- Vision and joined-up thinking – being of one mind on what is important;
- Virtue and joined-up action – being of one team when it comes to realising justice.

In a divided, and at times unjust world, the challenge which confronts all of us is to realise social unity and co-operation. We need to re-discover appropriate levels of unity of purpose and intent in a world of diversity and pluralism. The Nobel Peace Prize recipient, Elie Wiesel, has said: 'I don't like the word tolerance. Tolerance is degrading. Who am I to tolerate you? I would replace it with respect.'[6] In my view, at least three words stand out – learning, community and mutual respect – all of which working together can provide the basis for mutual care and shared well-being. Learning to live in satisfying relationships with others is the work of a lifetime and the greatest gift we can leave to our children is the example of learning and reciprocity based on right passion, vision and virtue. All of this is only possible through collective and shared responsibility recognising that we live in each other's shadow.

A few years ago, I found on the internet the following anonymous poem within a composite of responses to the question 'Why a learning organisation?'[7]

As I see it,
through the glass dimly (if not darkly),
we learn with the aim to live
more fully,
to become,
simply to contribute –

whether personally, communally, or
'organisationally' –
more of the world.

We learn
to live more fully
simply to contribute
more for the world.

We learn better
in communion
I think generally
than we do alone –
communion with the
whole world
and beyond the world
that we can see and touch and know
personally.

In learning in communion
WE have the simple hope
perhaps the real promise
of doing more
for the world
by being
more in communion
with the world,
and more.

And speaking personally,
as I see it,
that's why.

Notes

1. All of the views expressed in this paper are in personal capacity and do not necessarily represent the views of OECD or the Department of Education and Science in Ireland.
2. http://www.finegael.com/news/121699jb.htm
3. G. Veenstra, 'Social Capital and Health', 2001.
4. J. Abbott and T. Ryan, *The Unfinished Revolution*, 2000.
5. S. Knack, 'Trust, Associational Life and Economic Performance', 2001; S. Knack and P. Keefer, 'Does Social Capital Have an Economic Payoff? A Cross-Country Investigation', 1997
6. *The Prague Post*, October 24-30, 2001
7. The poem can be found at http://www.learning-org.com/WhyLO.html. See also http://www.learning-org.com Reproduced with permission of Richard Karash

References

Abbott, J. and Ryan, T., *The Unfinished Revolution*, Stafford: Network Educational Press Limited, 2000

Blanchflower, R.D.G. and Oswald, A.J., 'Well-being over Time in Britain and the USA', Working Paper No. 7487, National Bureau of Economic Research, 2000

Bohan, H. and Kennedy, G (eds), *Redefining Roles and Relationships*, Dublin: Veritas, 2001

DeToqueville, A., *Democracy in America*, New York: Doubleday, 1969

'Forum Voices', report of Forum 2000 meeting in Prague, *The Prague Post*, October 24-30, 2001

Fukuyama, F., *Trust: The Social Virtues and the Creation of Prosperity*, New York: The Free Press, 1995

Frey, B, 'Institutions and morale', in A. Ben-Ner and L. Puttnam (eds) *Economics, Values and Organisation*, Cambridge University Press, 1999

Helliwell, J.F. (ed), *The Contribution of Human and Social Capital to Sustained Economic Growth and Well-being: International Symposium Report*, Human Resources Development Canada and OECD, 2001

Hurlbert, J.S., Haines, V.A., and Beggs, J.J., 'Core networks and tie activation: What kinds of routine networks allocate resources and nonroutine situations', *American Sociological Review*, 65 (2000), 598-618

Knack, S., 'Trust, Associational Life and Economic Performance', in J.F. Helliwell (ed.), *The Contribution of Human and Social Capital to Sustained Economic Growth and Well-being: International*

Symposium Report, Human Resources Development Canada and OECD, 2001

Knack, S. and Keefer, P., 'Does Social Capital Have an Economic Payoff? A Cross-Country Investigation', *Quarterly Journal of Economics*, 112:4 (1997), 1251-1288

OECD, *The Well-Being of Nations: the Role of Human and Social Capital*, Paris, 2001

Putman, R., *Bowling Alone: The Collapse and Revival of American Community*, New York: Simon Schuster, 2000

Veenstra, G., 'Social capital and health', *Journal of Policy Research*, Spring 2001

VIEW FROM THE CHAIR

John Quinn

It was a long day. The conference theme may have been 'Is the Future my Responsibility?', but from 9 a.m. to 5 p.m. on Thursday November 8th the conference was going to be *my* responsibility. A daunting prospect. Guiding four speakers through the day, absorbing the issues, mediating the questions and above all facing six hundred eager delegates from a wide cross section of Irish Society – daunting wasn't the word! All that apart, my personal circumstances had changed dramatically in the preceding months. My beautiful wife had died suddenly in June. Outwardly I was calm, but inwardly I was in turmoil. Give me a hand out here, Olive, please.

Our keynote speaker was Charles Handy. I have known and admired him for sixteen years. A thinker, a doer and a wonderful communicator. Always a pleasure to watch him in action. The delivery, the metaphor and the marvellous use of the pause. How he invites you into his thinking. 'Elephants and Fleas' constituted the topic for the morning. Once again a wonderful metaphor. The elephants – those large, lumbering organisations that are now rapidly growing fragile and short lived, tending to gobble each other up. The fleas – the autonomous individuals who come in a number of guises – professional fleas, entrepreneurial fleas, occasional fleas, reluctant fleas. The view from the chair is fascinating. Six hundred people are hanging on Charles Handy's every word. I can tell it is not just the medium – it is the message. Handy's questions are hitting home. How much is enough? Where do I strike the balance in my life? What's it all about anyway? His suggestions as ever are challenging – and the prize? Happiness. What is happiness? We all have our definitions of that one. Inwardly I reflect that sometimes you have it and you don't realise you have it. Charles Handy turns to the Chinese for an answer – 'Something to work on, something to hope for, someone to love'. Amen. The Question and the Answer session becomes an armchair session. We had tried this before in the National Concert Hall and it had worked. It worked here too; it gave an ease and informality to the occasion. A woman from the audience later told me it was like 'having the two of you chatting in my sitting room'. We could have chatted all day but Charles has to catch a plane to New Zealand – and I am left with a tricky situation. Forty-five minutes to fill and an empty chair beside me. But it wasn't that tricky at all. The audience was energised and self-directing and, by the way, that chair wasn't empty at all, thanks to Olive.

So the visiting team played a blinder. How would the home team fare? It was an impressive line up. First came Anne Coughlan, a senior researcher with IBEC from the Elephant Sector! Anne used a lot of 'F' words – flexibility and family-friendly policies. They are key words in the struggle to juggle working lives, improve the quality of life and ultimately find a work/life balance. Her finely researched and well presented paper argued for the integration of a work-life strategy into a company's culture. Management need to be convinced of its worth, employees need to ease their worries about career prospects, status, the attitude of their colleagues. We are back to choices and Handy questions – What is enough? *What's it all about?*

2001 was the International Year of the Volunteer, so it was appropriate that our second speaker Freda Donoghue addressed the theme 'The Value of Volunteering', again as befitted someone who has written and researched extensively on her subject, Freda gave us a profile of the voluntary sector with clarity and precision. Who are the volunteers? Why do they do it? (And why do people not do it? – interesting that many had *never been asked*). What are the benefits to the individual, to society? Volunteering very obviously contributes to the building and the sustaining of society, contributes to social capital.

An obvious cue for our final speaker, Tom Healy, who as co-author of the OECD report *The Well Being of Nations: the Role of Human and Social Capital* was more well placed to address us on human and social capital. We may not be 'bowling alone' a la Robert Puttnam but we should not be complacent either, or we could end up 'hurling alone'. I can see Harry Bohan's brow furrowing intensely at the thought of what that would mean for Clare Hurling! Social capital, we are told, will make us 'happy, healthy, learned and wealthy'. What are we waiting for? Well you see it doesn't just happen. It needs to be worked on, be properly designed. Gradually there comes roundedness to the day's deliberations. Economic well-being is not the total of human well being, we are talking Gross National *Happiness*. There's that word again – happiness – and vision and trust – Handy's words.

The home team sparks a flood of questions. They have done us proud; a woman later says to me of Tom Healy – 'A new star is born'.

Five o'clock. I am exhausted but relieved and happy that the day has gone well. It was a long day. I can look forward to relaxing at the conference dinner. And guess what? There is an empty chair at my dinner table. Thanks, Olive.

WHERE DOES RESPONSIBILITY START?

Carmel Foley

A couple of weeks ago, on my way into work one morning, I was listening to Marian Finucane's programme on RTÉ radio. Her guest was Angela Phelan, a popular social columnist with the *Irish Independent* who had just published a book about shopping in New York. Apparently, there are wonderful bargains to be had in designer labels if you know the right suburban malls and warehouses to go to. Frankly, up to that moment, I didn't. But now I do.

Anyway, in a nutshell, the basic advice is: don't shop on 5th Avenue. Go instead to the mall at the Woodbury Commercial Centre, or the mall at Jersey Gardens. Got that? Woodbury and Jersey Gardens New Yorkers will tell you scornfully that only tourists are dumb enough to shop on 5th Avenue. Angela Phelan is not dumb. Blonde maybe, but she knows New York. By way of example, Angela cited a Chanel dress for sale in a boutique on 5th Avenue for $3,000 that she saw later in the day, the same dress, marked down in a Woodbury Mall for a mere $500. Two and a half thousand dollars saved for a $10 dollar trip across town on a bus from the Port Authority.

And nobody had to ask: 'Where or what is the Port Authority?' Nobody even had to query the location of Woodbury Mall or Jersey Centre. The crucial information as far as Marian, who's a very astute broadcaster and interviewer, and I presume, consumer, was concerned was that Aer Lingus would get you to New York return for a mere £169 return and that three nights in a four star hotel had been slashed to a mere $369. And, oh yes, you could get your thousands of dollars worth of bargain-mall goodies back through Irish customs, no questions asked. All the girls do. Every weekend.

All very nice and comfortable and exciting for nice middle-class women at the top of their careers in journalism and broadcasting. And Flo McSweeney, a jazz singer, also in studio, she'd been to New York last year when the flight cost £600. And she could tell us more about bargains and malls, and hey, New York's a fun city. And even with the pound at parity with the dollar, or *whaddeveh*, it all made sense, and was great fun.

And then, lest we all get into a dudgeon about the privileges of the middle classes, and the life-style of jazz singers, on comes a woman caller with a Dublin working-class accent. She too is a regular visitor to the Big Apple. And yes, the shopping is great if you know where to go. And she and all her mates know exactly where to go now that she's been there several times. But she thinks it a bit much to have to pay up to $10 for a beer, and on top of that a dollar tip with every round.

But just in case you think the mall is a new concept to Irish consumers, let me disabuse you of that one. Recently, I was looking through the book of Dorothea Lange's wonderful photographs taken here in Clare at just this time of year, in 1954. Dorothea was an American professional photographer who had specialised in recording American rural life during the Depression. She has one terrific picture taken in the mall in Ennis, a very different Mall to what we would expect in New

York – but still a market place, a place where people buy and sell. The photograph is of a rural market, with men in stout overcoats buying cabbage plants from a stack laid out on the street. This mall in Ennis is a warm image of what we might think of as De Valera's 'frugal comfort'. But the kids reared on those cabbage plants, now with their own children reared and possibly put through college, can take a plane from their nearby international airport and, five hours later, buy Chanel in another mall in New York. Indeed, when one looks carefully at Dorothea Lange's Clare collection of 1954, what one sees in this county, and in this town of Ennis, is not poverty, but limited choice. Fifty years later that choice has become limitless.

But back in Dublin, with all this reverie resounding in my head, I get to my office, just a few minutes late and the top sheet of paper on my desk has a question across the top: 'Is the Future My Responsibility?' And then it says 'Ms Carmel Foley, "Where Does Responsibility Start?".' Well, a strong cup of coffee, that's where we'll really start. But let us just put that theme to one side for a moment while we deal with the present.

First, a memo from a colleague, the Minister's office wants to know what we're doing about prices and people being ripped off with the euro conversion. Memo to self: do not, even jokingly, write back to the Minister asking is that prices on 5th Avenue, Jersey Mall or Henry Street? Reply instead saying newspaper accounts are greatly exaggerated and remind the Minister respectfully that it is Government and EU policy that we are committed to competition as the price determinant.

And while journalists on the Marian Finucane show can merrily accept that the punt is at parity with the dollar (which it's not), do not, under any circumstances write to the Minister saying: all retail outlets are converting the punt at the legally binding €1.27.

And then I open a letter from a TD indignant on behalf of a constituent who was charged £3.50 for a pint of Budweiser in a Dublin nightclub at 4 o'clock in the morning, and yet the constituent got the same pint of Budweiser in his local in Drumcondra for £2.50 when he started out the previous afternoon. And when are we going to investigate these nightclubs? Then I put down the cup of coffee and reach again for this document that asks: How do we take responsibility for a self-driven society? And specifically: Where does responsibility start?

Does it start with the individual, with the community, with business, with government?

All of you here are aware that we live in an age of consumption. Indeed with steadily fewer people feeling the need to fight ideological wars, to protest or even to vote, it could be argued that the expression of consumer choice through economic transactions has become a defining political activity of our times.

Some of you may bemoan this fact, but agree with it or not, popular democracy, or the exercise of choice, is most often nowadays practised in the marketplace, not the polling booth. Whether for Chanel or for cabbage plants, flying Aer Lingus or Ryanair, people are voting with their wallets. Indeed one could argue that the kind of society we have is, in many ways, dictated by consumer choice, the ultimate in government by the people.

But, in a market place, in exercising consumer choice, there can be a sharp imbalance of power between vendor and buyer. The dice can often be heavily loaded against the consumer. The buyer must still beware. So, we look for ways to tilt the balance back. We look for interventions, and these interventions can be personal, competitive or regulatory.

The dominant ideological view at governmental and European Union level is that effective competition is the best form of market regulation. But I don't need to tell you that in an imperfect world competition is often imperfect, and not always effective – intervention, through regulation, will always be necessary. But even if we had the finest regulatory laws in the world, they will never truly meet their legislative and social aspirations unless people, consumers, are prepared to complain, to demand, and to refuse. Consumer responsibility starts at the checkout, in what you might call: a counter revolution.

There is an extraordinary conventional view that Irish consumers don't complain half enough. And that if we were to complain more, and kick up more of a racket, the customer, *mirabile dictu*, might start to be right – for a change. And if we raised our voices and stamped our feet often enough everything in the marketplace would improve: pub service, shop service, hotel service – all would be much, much better.

I see evidence of this spirit of complaint all the time. Last year my own office had no less than 21,000 calls from consumers seeking advice on how to more effectively fight their corner. The issues that topped the enquiry list were: clothing, motorcars, holidays, furniture, electrical goods and computers. Armed with the information we supplied to them, many of these callers sorted out their own problems. But this 21,000 is only the tip of the iceberg of complainants. These are the people who have failed to resolve their difficulties themselves, and quite rightly, are now looking for the assistance that my office can offer them.

We carried out just over 2,000 investigations. I would like here, again, to refer to the possible imbalance of power between buyer and seller. I take into account here, also, an understanding that in commercial relationships, as in many others, information or knowledge is power. And what I mean here is that, at the point of purchase, the consumer should have the required information to make what we call an informed decision. But that information, sometimes legally required information, is either not available, or in some cases misrepresented or downright dishonest. So that, of those 2,000 investigations, nearly 60 per cent of them covered misleading information, price display, or product safety.

As I said, we had over 21,000 complainants last year. These complaints, made to us, I would contend, are part of the process of consumers taking individual responsibility. But we can only speculate on the hundreds of thousands of consumers who make their protest known at point of sale, or later, and in doing so take responsibility for their own commercial relationships.

I must say that I have always had difficulty with the clichéd notion that we're too timid to complain or to bargain about quality or price. That so-called timidity has not been much in evidence in my experience. I mean, how many of you recall, as I do, when you were children that dreaded moment out shopping with your parents when your father or mother got stuck into a shop assistant or waiter. And you looked on mortified: 'Ah Ma', or 'Ah Da', 'Come on' you pleaded, in the vain hope that this shameful, social torture could end quickly. And how many of you, so many years later, as you yourselves are just about getting stuck into the shopkeeper or manager, hear this little, perhaps slightly more aggressive, voice beside you pleading: 'Ah Ma', or 'Ah Da, get a life'.

I mentioned Marian Finucane's radio programme earlier. It is interesting to note the degree to which the media are now engaged in the consumer debate, how our memories of consumer issues can be dominated by what we've heard on radio talk shows or 'access programmes' as they are sometimes called. One of my first memories of consumer complaints, this was some time before I took up the position of Director of Consumer Affairs, was when listening to the Gay Byrne Show one day. There was this woman from Dublin telling Gay about a carpet she had bought in a city carpet showroom. She paid something like £400 for it, which was a lot of money at the time. But when the carpet was delivered she found a huge discolouration in the centre of it. So she got on to the carpet shop to get her money back and they simply refused, point blank, and were really stroppy about it. Anyway, she persisted, and eventually got her money. 'So how did you manage it?' says Gay, 'Did you send them a solicitor's letter, or what?' 'No,' says the woman, 'my three brothers, now they're very big heavy fellas Gay, they went in and just had a chat with them. You know what I mean?'

Yes, we all know exactly what she meant. However, not all of us have the three big heavy brothers. And even if we had, it is not the way we wish to resolve consumer issues in a civilised society.

That's why consumer protection is now a fundamental part of our laws of contract and of trading; much in the manner developed in Europe and the United States over the past 30 years. Consumer protection is a significant political issue, as we have seen in the issue of financial regulation, the price of drinks, advertising for air flights, and policing the introduction of the euro. In practically every area of consumer/provider relationships there is a body of legislation to protect the consumer's interest. Not all of this legislation is entirely up to the task for which it was intended; and changing circumstances can make laws seem dated. But the unstoppable trend is for greater protection. And such is the demand for this protection that consumer issues are now very important political issues. I suspect that if one were to get the appearance figures from *Morning Ireland*, you would find that Minister Tom Kitt, who is responsible for Consumer Affairs in government, would be among the top ten.

But you have to ask: what's new about all this? After all, weights and measures have been around for an awful long time. The expression, 'Never mind the width, feel the quality', didn't come about today or yesterday. Product safety has been here since we first learnt to light fire with a flint, and cut timber with a stone axe. What's new of course is the complexity of our choices and of the products that are available to us. There is a difference between today's mall in Woodbury, New York, and the 1950s mall in Ennis, County Clare.

All of this legislation is terribly important. It sets standards, it protects, it creates a legal framework within which the consumer can get satisfaction, or get their money back. Mostly it attempts to prevent problems before the business transaction takes place, with a legal fall-back for when things go wrong. But knowing that the law is on your side won't do anything for your temper on a Saturday night if you're sitting in a restaurant facing an overcooked Beef Wellington and a bottle of red that would be better off sprinkled over on the chips. And knowing that you can ring my office on Monday morning to get a leaflet on the small claims court will not soothe your bile; nor will it restore normal diplomatic relations with your beloved across the table.

So, what do you do? Do you complain? And will the hassle of complaining, and the embarrassment, spoil your evening even more? Or do you internalise it all, and just fume? And say 'Yes, thank you' when the waiter or manager asks was everything all right? And do you then grimly, and silently, leave the restaurant resolved never to cross that threshold again?

This is not just a peculiarly Irish problem. A friend of mine who works for an American airline tells me that Japanese customers never complain. If they are unhappy with the service you just never see them again. Swedes, on the other hand, complain loud, long and often, and just love to come back for more to the same. But, can I say at this point, my advice to you, if you are faced with poor service or a faulty product, is to holler long and loud, and as embarrassingly as possible, until you get satisfaction. And to hell with the blushes. Can you do it? Of course you can. People like you who in your daily lives organise, negotiate, manage your jobs, manage your family needs, manage your finances – you are all well prepared for fighting your corner in the marketplace. And I bet many of you are already doing it to great effect.

My own office had no less than 21,000 calls last year. But sorting consumer problems is not just the responsibility of my

office, or of the aggrieved customer. It is primarily the
responsibility of the service provider. Now some business
people will see this simply as an additional burden in their haste
to make a profit. But let me say, in these more consumer
conscious days, that attitude is a fast track to the bankruptcy
courts.

For a moment, let me put you in the position of the
manager, or the proprietor, or the service provider who has an
angry, never-to-come-back client heading fuming out the door
of your restaurant or shop.

You've just lost a customer. After all you've done; after all
your effort; after all your dreams and schemes. You've spent a
fortune, you've spent years of your life developing a restaurant,
or a product, or a service – and you've just lost a customer.
You've had every expensive marketer, advertiser, interior
decorator, banker – every solicitor and accountant that
borrowed money can buy – and you've just lost a customer.
And what's even worse, is that you don't even know it yet!

That customer who never speaks of you again, or who never
buys from you again, is an opportunity lost and an investment
wasted. Maybe if your customer confronted you with their
rage or their knowledge of consumer law, at least you could
respond and defend yourself and make sure you get it right the
next time. But if your customer is employing the brutal law of
the marketplace and voting with their feet, there is no second
time round, you have got to get your consumer awareness, and
your product, right from the start.

The picture I've painted might lead you to believe that this is
a terrifying time to be a service provider. Between picky
customers and the increased public profile of offices like my
own, it may seem as if businesses have a whole new set of
demands placed on them. With that can come a whole new set
of fears; a kind of siege mentality.

That is certainly one way of looking at it. But there is
another and it is about partnership. The most progressive and

successful businesses in the world are increasingly pursuing relationships with customers that are based on partnership rather than the adversarial model; on creating an 'us' relationship rather than having 'thems'; of creating a sense of loyalty in their customers so that they become advocates rather than mere clients.

And this relationship of partnership is also about trust. Trust is a bit like good drama, it requires a certain amount of suspension of disbelief. We are asked to believe that our meat does not contain growth promoters; that our milk is free of harmful bacteria. We believe that a product contains only what it says on the packet. We have faith we will not be electrocuted when we use a hair dryer or food mixer. We trust that the tyres on our cars will keep us safe within certain tolerances. We trust, but only up to a point; and not in all circumstances. We, the consumers, have learned over time, and sometimes from bitter experience, that *caveat emptor*, the Roman warning, 'Let the buyer beware', translates pointedly to modern tongues and modern times. So consumers enter the market place with trust tempered by prudence, and where necessary, by law.

This trust is central to the approach of the European Union in our changeover from our present currencies to the euro. All of the countries have decided to trust the sellers of the marketplace to manage the euro conversion honestly, and not seek to benefit unfairly from the changeover. There is no sanctioning law in place to punish miscreants. Nor is there any law enforcing compliance. What we have is an expectation that the process of trust is so embedded in our commercial life, that we can depend on business to comply. In Ireland this compliance is evidenced in businesses signing up to the euro logo and displaying it prominently in their premises. The logo is a badge of honour; a pledge to convert to the euro honestly and transparently, and without seeking gain or advantage. By any standards it is a remarkable pledge. It is also a remarkable act of faith by government and consumer. It is a groundbreaking opportunity for business to be a driving force for responsibility in society. And I believe that the ultimate outcome of this act of faith, of this pledge of honour, will colour the development of consumer relations in Ireland, and in Europe for many years to come.

However, if this partnership of business and consumer, of honour and trust, is seen to falter or fail, there can still be recourse to the coercive authority of law and of government. It is not a path that either I or the government wish to tread but, in a matter so important as the introduction of a new, European currency, you can be certain that deviant behaviour by the few will not be allowed to tarnish this major move. Government too has its responsibilities.

The notion of partnership has played a large part in Ireland's economic planning in recent years. Governments, trade unions, employers, farmers, and representatives of the disadvantaged, have negotiated common economic and societal goals. The concept of partnership in the relationship between business and consumer is a sophisticated and long-term view of the customer. And it's quite new to Irish business. For all their good intentions of giving good service, some businesses trim when it comes to delivery. We sometimes refer to it as 'a quick buck'. The modern consumer is too sophisticated for the 'quick buck' mentality and prefers the philosophy of partnership, even advocacy.

This new philosophy requires that instead of fearing the new sophisticated consumer, businesses should view this sophistication as an opportunity. Pleasing a consumer is not an annoyance or an irritation. It is in fact a new and exciting way for companies to gain a sustainable advantage over their rivals. It's a new form of competition. And it's new form of consumer consciousness.

Now, with regard to where responsibility starts at community level, there are some observations I would like to make. I know that, at an individual consumer level, there has been a great leap in confidence and consumer awareness. But I have to say, that at a national level, at what you might call an organised national level, popular organisations have been strangely quiet on the issue of consumer affairs. Neither community organisations, women's organisations, trade unions, nor regional groups seem to see themselves as having a vested interest in consumer issues. Unlike farmers, bankers, travel agents, supermarkets, shopkeepers, and industrialists, all of whom will arrive in delegations to my office, and at government offices, and be seen all over the media whenever they see their end of the consumer affairs relationship being affected. I have seldom, if ever, been visited by a trade union delegation or a community group in this regard. And what this produces, along with some other absences, is a serious imbalance in the consumer affairs debate. And let me say that I would welcome it if the trade unions and other national and regional community groups were to engage more actively on the consumer front.

Ireland is different to other European countries in that there is very little consumer activism at a community or organised level. I mean community, not necessarily just in its geographical sense, but also as community of interest. For instance there are no specialist representative groups for consumers of telecoms, or house purchasing, or financial services, or travel and leisure, or health services, or child care, or food quality and safety. And I have to tell you that I think that such absence of specialist, active interest and campaigning is seriously missed in the consumer area. My own office would greatly welcome the arrival of such specialist community groups, and I would be greatly disposed to assisting them in start-ups and development.

There is no doubt that the Celtic Tiger has put a lot more money in everybody's pocket and has created merry tunes on an awful lot of cash registers. Furthermore, I believe that this much more sophisticated and aware population of ours has become adept at spending well and spending thoughtfully. But there is an aspect of consumer/provider relationships that I have to say concerns me. And that is what I call: 'acceptance by inertia'. It will be familiar to you as the inertia brought on by the dense detail and small print of a mobile phone contract. These are the dense details that convert into those large bills that you may not have expected, nor are you in a position to afford. There is nothing illegal about these contracts, but it seems to me that an active telecoms users group could do a lot to bring greater clarity and understandable transparency to this area.

Similarly, I have yet to be convinced that the supermarket system of pricing on the shelf, rather than on the package, really works to the advantage of the consumer. I am concerned that a number of surveys have shown that most shoppers haven't the faintest idea of individual prices of everyday items bought in their supermarkets. How many people check each price on the shelf tag? In their haste to get through the checkout, how many of these prices are remembered? How many of these prices are then tallied against the receipt? Not many, I guess. It's that old inertia again. Presented with that combination of convenience and complexity, in our already busy lives, we no longer know the cost of anything – whatever about its value.

And we find that the same inertia hits the consumer consciousness of many people making expensive purchases. People buying new cars will sign themselves blindly into very unfavourable financial contracts without even checking what exactly it is they are signing. Consumers are signing up for easily acquired financial loans without ever checking the small print that lists the penalty clauses that will kick in when they fail to meet their payment dates. This inertia may very well hit them hard if ever the bank comes to demand their money back – plus the penalties.

Vigilance is as important in consumer relations as it is in all other areas of public life. What I fear is that our vigilance is being dulled by convenience. Our inertia then becomes something we pay for – literally in cash. Our inertia strips us of our critical responsibility to take charge of our affairs.

I started by recounting to you a discussion I heard on a radio programme. Radio programmes, particularly access radio where listeners can call in and tell their story or air their grievances have become a major part of the public dialogue on all matters. Ring Joe, ring Marian, ring Pat, ring Gerry or Eamon, has become a common response to dealing with many of the daily difficulties and scandals that life throws our way. And often what is happening when listeners or consumers ring in to these programmes is that they are taking public action, personal and public responsibility for their own protection, and for the protection of others. Phone-in programmes have become a serious wake-up call for many a recalcitrant service provider, and a knight in shining armour and an empowerment for many a hapless consumer.

The committed interest of our newspapers to consumer affairs, with many of the national papers having consumer correspondents is evidence of a new interest, a new awareness of this empowerment, and new recognition that not only is the customer always right, but that the customer has a right to be right. But rights, as we know, can be diluted, evaded, or even ignored. My job, as Director of Consumer Affairs, is to ensure that they are not. The job of Government is to provide the statutory framework of protection. The press, radio and television will throw light on how we perform and how we interact.

But in the first instance, consumer relations emerge from a private commercial contract between seller and buyer, an exchange of promise and trust. Both parties have the primary responsibility to make that relationship work. The everyday success of the contract is just as important to the fabric of life in Ennis as it is on 5th Avenue. So let the buyer be aware, and let the seller beware.

CÉIFIN
AN INTERNATIONAL INSTITUTE FOR VALUES-LED CHANGE

Harry Bohan

The story behind Céifin began in 1997, when a few of us started to examine the extraordinary changes taking place in Ireland. We have now reached the stage where we are beginning to do something about understanding the issues involved and implementing some tentative solutions.

At the outset we felt we should spend some quiet time in reflecting on what we were about. And so we touched into what we considered a deep well in that we made serious and regular contact with a contemplative order.

All worthwhile initiatives begin with debate. However, we have been determined from the outset that the debate would result in a programme of action – a programme of action that would touch the lives of people. The work above begins where people are!

Many of you have been with us through the debates of the past three years as we examined the issues facing 'Our Society in the New Millennium'. As the rapid rate of change threatened to engulf society, we posed the question – 'Are We Forgetting Something?' While it was obvious that we were in danger of ditching many of the values that had sustained us for generations, people like John Drew, who is the director of an Institute for the study of change at Durham University, assured us that change could indeed be managed. We reached agreement that people need balance in their lives. This led us at our second conference to look at 'Working Towards Balance'. This conference underlined the importance of restoring the balance between ideology and technology, between the demands of family life and the demands of the workplace and between powerlessness and an ethics system that is rooted in people being given and taking responsibility. In order to achieve this there is a need for 'Redefining Roles and Relationships'. At last year's conference we debated how best this could be done.

This debate to which many of you have contributed has featured the cream of national and international speakers. It has been broadened to the wider community by the publication of the papers from each conference in book form. This year you will see also a video and audio-tape of the entire proceedings of last year's event as well as a specially edited interactive CD ROM aimed at schools, libraries and other educational outlets. Practical research has begun into the links between work and lifestyle and where action can be taken to ensure the balance. The family has undergone enormous change. Funding has been sourced for a pilot study on the family to be undertaken in County Clare in the coming months. It is intended that this will lead to a major national study on the state of the family throughout Ireland. So we have a programme of action.

The more we have delved into the debate and examined the issues over the past three years the more we have become convinced of the need for an Institute for Values-Led Change. People value their freedom above all else. Freedom is central to our lives, but unless that human freedom has goals which stretch it, unless there are ideals and involvement for ideals, there can be a spiritual and emotional vacuum which adversely affects both individual and community.

In the midst of an 'information society' there is thirst of the spirit and for many a search for the meaning of life. This search is now evident in many areas of Irish society. I believe we need less information and more confirmation.

There are indications now in our western scientific world that the pillars of sacredness have been destablised. The unspeakable human barbarism, the wilful environmental degradation and the widespread suborning of ethical principles of the twentieth century has left even the Churches clutching for the straws of moral security.

We are now witnessing the passing of a whole tradition, *the end of an era*. There is a *serious disconnecting* of people, particularly young people, from all kinds of institutions, family, community, organised religion, and so on. There are indications that a generation of Irish people are growing up not so much in an atmosphere of unbelief but of non-belief. We may be the best fed, best housed, best schooled, most-employed generation ever to have lived in Ireland, but there is a *feeling of emptiness* about modern life for many young people that expresses itself in *detachment*, in an absence of real commitment and in a serious dependency on alcohol and drugs.

Many powerful institutions of the past are finding it difficult to adapt in the face of great change. The inclination is to hold on to power, self-preservation and legitimisation. Every organisation has its own mission statement, its own set of values and its own turf to protect. Very many such organisations are, however, running out of gimmicks to motivate people and are discovering that what really motivates people is that which gives deep meaning and purpose to their jobs and in their lives generally.

Over the last few years we have been experiencing events, almost on a daily basis, locally and globally that shock us. Many of these are to do with a disregard for human life that began with a disregard for the sacred and then creation. In a sense this is a time of trial for western people.

Will we continue to propound solely the values of a material society or will we now take stock of the need for spiritual (in the widest possible sense), emotional and powerful community and social factors to be built into our *new matrix for progress*? We have lost the contemplative dimension of our lives. In every person a certain balance or harmony has to be achieved – but in our western world the technological, competitive, aggressive powers, often leading to violence, have become so dominant that we will have to pause, reflect and search as to how we can bring about radical changes. The limitations of western science and capitalism have become more evident. The future may be germinating today, not in a board-room in London, or an office in Washington, or in the stock exchange in Tokyo, but in some outpost of the Middle East or in the grim foothills of Peru or in a back street in Calcutta.

We see Céifin as providing the opportunity for people, individuals and groups, to search and to reflect. Most people have an inner core set of values, but the stresses and strains of modern-day life may have obscured them or rendered them temporarily non-operative. Change and our ability to adapt wisely, rationally and effectively to change are at the heart of what we are and what we seek to become. Nowadays we have institutes for this and institutes for that – however, none of these are dedicated to an understanding of change and an understanding of values.

In our brochure for Céifin the question is posed: 'How is a National Development Plan more important than a National Strategy of Values?' *How indeed?*

During the past twelve months we have given considerable thought to what Céifin can offer, to those who will use it, to where it will be located, to what the building will be like, to what it will cost. We spent many hours and days wondering what we should call the Institute. We wanted a name that was both unique and that had significance. When we needed inspiration we decided on Céifin, a name derived from Céibhfhionn – the Celtic goddess of inspiration.

We have undertaken a huge amount of background work in putting support structures in place. Building and funding committees have been working for several months and wonderful support has been received for the idea from many quarters. One has only to look at the list of people on the back of your brochure who have lent their names as patrons, trustees and associate members.

We have no doubt that the Céifin project is timely. Ireland is experiencing a cultural revolution. We have had three generations of post-colonisation and we now have the first generation of post-clericalism. How can we be sure that the rapid erosion of one structure, heretofore held largely unaccountable, will not simply be replaced by others? People don't trust structures because trust has been broken. The concept of 'active trust' underpins new forms of governance. Are we as a people ready to take on this responsibility? Are we as a community ready to enter this new questioning dispensation? What is the meaning of the people of God for the upcoming generation? Are we ready to insist on wholesale and widespread participation in the decision processes? Do we agree that debate should come before decisions (i.e. policies)? Are we prepared to fight as vigorously for the inclusion of human/spiritual elements in future developments as we are for the physical elements? Are we prepared to take our place in this new national development process? All of this must begin with a listening process.

In recent months the world has experienced a massive outburst of comment on the relations between the West and the rest of the world. It is becoming clear that fundamentalism is not something confined to Islamic civilisation. The fact that the dogma in the West is now more secular than spiritual does not mean the same mind-sets do not continue to flourish, as rigid, dogmatic and cruel as ever.

If anything good is to come out of the events of September 11th it may be that they will induce us to apply our critical capacity to our own value system. Céifin will encourage every group – religious, political, commercial, educational – to reflect on their values and understand that the search for harmony and the building of relationships now poses a far more formidable challenge than achieving perpetual economic growth.

We are now, in theory, in a self-driven society. *The future is our responsibility. This cultural revolution is real* and will not pass. *The path of reconstruction must begin with search.* This is why we need the Institute. There is an urgency about this. We have been through an era of compliance. We have entered an era of search. We must do this together in partnership. If we are to manage change, manage the future, respond to real needs, we must begin with the people – where they are.

We are aware of the size of the task we are taking on in setting up Céifin. We are determined however that it will be unique and that it will make a difference.

We believe that individual change will lead to organisational change and to societal change. We will need the help and support of very many people, active and passive, in order to achieve this goal – but we know that it will be worth it in the end.

FROM PAPER TO PRACTICE

AN OVERVIEW OF THE CÉIFIN PROCESS

Kate Ó Dubhchair

What I want to do in this paper is to explain the concept of Céifin in a practical way – why now, what will it do, what is the Céifin Process, what difference will it make.

But first of all I want to say a couple of personal things about my own involvement. I didn't get to the first conference here entitled 'Are We Forgetting Something?', but I remember well being deeply moved by a conversation with a friend who did. When I asked her was what it was about she said it was about putting the soul back into society. I read the book and vowed if there was a follow-up I'd be there. Before that happened, however, I found myself sharing a platform with Fr Harry Bohan on the anniversary of the Omagh tragedy, each of us speaking on renewal and regeneration. We talked long into the night, discovering shared views and concerns and a mutual passion for people and the importance of community. He invited me to join the Céifin Applied Research Committee, I accepted and in November 1999 I literally drove through hell and high water to attend a meeting of that body and the conference.

I suppose realistically my involvement might have continued at that level if the rest of my life had continued as normal. But it didn't and as some of you know early in 2000 I took on the battle with cancer. A big wake-up call, a crisis of course but also an opportunity for change. I had already planned a sabbatical and I took that, but, with the cooperation of good friends in Missouri, rearranged my plans to concentrate on Céifin. My belief in the inevitability of the initiative has grown with every step of the journey from then to now. I have made the difficult decision to step out of the security of the university, become both more of a character and more of a flea, and devote all my energy and resources to Céifin. I know without a doubt that this is the best use I can make of my time and the best contribution I can make and I consider myself lucky to have the chance to do it.

Fr Harry spoke of a cultural revolution and he is right. Civilisations pass through stages of growth and decline just like each of us. You only have to think of the rise and fall of the Roman Empire. These stages are like the seasons – spring, summer, autumn and winter – and there are recognisable signs of each season. In Ireland, as part of the larger western civilisation, we are clearly, at best, in the autumn of this cycle. Cynicism, discord and bureaucratic complexity are all blatantly familiar. History would tell us that if we simply continue as we are we will head for disaster and the complete breakdown of society. This is not a point of debate: what we have here is a crisis.

Change is not a neutral process. In the face of change we need to protect the things we value. As Paddy Walley notes in his book on Ireland in the twenty-first century: 'Values must be applied in relationship to change. There are ... vital aspects of human culture that need to be protected in the process of change.'

These values are particularly threatened when a society takes choice into its own hands. Then the forces of aggression, dominance, individualism and injustice come to the fore. Increased choice certainly frees and enriches but it also makes us less secure in who we are and more isolated from one another. Traditional Ireland bound conformity and belonging close together. Much of our disconnecting has come from a rejection of conformity and that is fine. Most people would support a society more tolerant of diversity. But that puts the onus back on each of us to choose our identity, our social reality. Social cohesion and social capital have always been a strength of this country. We are 'people people'. Social cohesion and social capital can no longer be regarded as a given, they now need to be created through choice. As John Hume and Charles Handy suggested, this is the major social·challenge of the new millennium. This is what Céifin is about – support for each of us, an investment in belonging, an investment in the social glue that holds us together, investment in the people of Ireland.

Let me say that you are right all those times when you have you said to yourself: 'There must be more to life than this'. Stuck in a traffic jam on a Friday evening, crawling, or putting effort into meeting deadlines and jumping hurdles, only to find the pace and height endlessly increasing.

You're right when you ask: what's the world coming to? When someone drives at 60 miles an hour down a pedestrian street and mows down 10 people. Or, God help us, when thousands of innocent people lose their lives in a single act of terrorism.

You're right to question what is happening around us when millions of ecstasy tablets are consumed in the name of entertainment and happiness and when it is estimated that we all watch 25,000 advertisements per week without even knowing it.

But saying it won't make it better. This isn't someone else's problem. We can't expect our leaders to shoulder all the responsibility. We can't look to traditional institutions and structures for a fix. The majority of them are totally bogged down in their own internal crisis management. Bureaucracy has them on their knees. No, there is no one else. We are it: you, me. One by one we must take charge, one by one we must restore balance. This is our legacy to our children and our children's children. As Kelly Andrews of the US Labour Department said, 'The future is made in the present.'

The vision Céifin sets out to achieve is a future of harmonious living, authentic relationships – balance, a society where the individual lives with a sense of purpose and responsibility.

The Céifin Process starts and ends with people on the ground, people as individuals in everyday life. It is a three stage process. We start by listening to Change in Practice, change as it is being experienced, we build on that by reflecting, questioning and searching, and then we support the response, the action. To date we have developed eight activities within this cycle.

The first, and arguably, most important, addresses the need to draw a baseline, not on a macro, economic level, but the real picture of real people's lives, a social baseline. This is where Céifin has started. Through a panel of skilled facilitators who will work with us on this throughout the country we are reaching out to those who are living in the new Ireland.

Our first two baseline studies reflect major issues for the Ireland of today and tomorrow. Planning is a widely recognised issue. Everywhere you go in Ireland you see new settlements of private housing dropped into the countryside. The people who live here have a right to be proud of their homes, but it is a development without a heart. Residents share only a common address and no common unity. And worse, oftentimes it is a development that changes the whole social dynamic of the village or town it edges onto. For our first baseline study we are going to work with the people living in such a typical settlement and those living alongside in more traditional housing arrangements. What are their hopes, expectations, reactions, worries? How do they see their collective identity? Have they a sense of collective purpose? What do they want to change? Who do they need to work with to make those changes? I want to emphasise that this is no 'goldfish bowl community study'. Each group that we work with will be first of all doing something for themselves, but with the added value of helping society as a whole. Céifin, as Charles Handy explained, is Socratic. Céifin doesn't presume to supply the answers – it will help to raise the questions and uncover the alternatives. The people on the ground will take the study in whatever way they see fit.

Diversity is also a major challenge in the new Ireland. 'The Ireland of today' is more diverse than ever before. How do we cope with it? Are we 'Ireland of the Welcomes' or was that just about tourists? Will we just exploit immigrants as a resource or 'ghettoise' them at a safe distance? Three thousand immigrant babies will be born next year in Dublin. Are these Irish children?

Through Céifin we will consider these issues in partnership with a community. Céifin will help both sides hear each other's story, to get a real fix on what needs to be done and set about doing it.

The results of these studies and others like them will help build the big picture. They can't be one-off exercises. Through Céifin Advisory Panels we will bring insights to our host communities from others experiencing the same changes and we will feed back the lessons learned so that advances can be replicated and built upon. The findings, the issues identified by the people, will form the Céifin Research Agenda.

Céifin is about values-led change and so it will take a role in facilitating people to move to a values-led approach to their area. Fr Harry spoke of the Corporate Network. This is one example of a group who come together regularly to discuss values-led change, to debate on shared values and to put those values into practice. This model is totally transferable. Later this month we will start a similar process with religious and we have already begun it with teachers and parents. We are also developing a Mentoring Network, asking those who already have some experience of initiating and maintaining values-led change to join Céifin, share their experience and help others.

Those first three activities take place out there on the ground and they are crucial – they drive the Céifin Process.

Central to making change is the need for us individually and collectively to take stock – to take time out. Many organisations (including the Government and the Church) have recognised the need for 'away' days. This is part of the answer to 'Why can Céifin not be attached to a university or be a virtual institution'. There are sound reasons for the proposed purpose-built building and site, both of which will be part of the Céifin experience. As Stephen Covey, author of *The 7 Habits of Highly Effective People*, describes it, we all have a circle of influence. We underestimate the importance of that influence. Anita Roddick, in her new book *Take It Personally: How Globalisation Affects You and Powerful Ways to Challenge It*, puts it succinctly: 'If you think you are too small to make a difference go to bed with a mosquito'. If we consciously minimise our influence we abdicate our responsibility.

Each of us can make the difference. In Céifin we are currently putting together a clearly defined programme – 'Time for Change' – which we are offering to people as a vehicle they can use to pause, to reflect and to act. Ultimately this will run continuously and multiple groups will be run concurrently. We will be continually building the big picture of societal change in Ireland and sharing it with the people so that they, in turn, can develop individually and thus there will be roll-on organisational transformation

This is the core of Céifin. We are asking people to pause for three days, to invest three days in themselves and in the future of this country. Day 1 starts with that wider picture – a deepening of our understanding of societal change. Day 2 is a personal exploration of values. For each individual that has to start with thoughtful identification of what is important to him/her. What principles underpin your life, what values do you want to show up in your behaviour? How do these values apply to your personal life and to your work life or your community life?

Day 3 is forward planning. If this is the way I want to do business or relate, how can I make it happen in the real world? Look at your circle of influence. Who do you come in contact with? At what points do you have choice in your behaviour? Where are you prepared to take responsibility? What needs to happen to carry this through?

Every conversation we have had indicates a huge demand for this, a huge need. We are already having to build up a six-month waiting list of those who want to use Céifin. I want to emphasise that this is a resource for everyone. It is non-denominational, multi-sectoral, non-prescriptive and intended to be totally inclusive. Ultimately we plan to have several groups at a time taking Time for Change and coming together to interact, to see their world through eachothers' eyes: bankers with communities, companies and families, teachers and parents, teachers and pupils, religious and lay, politicians and the man on the street.

Céifin is an international institute and one of the strengths of that will be realised through debate. In the spring we will begin our Changing World/Changing Lives seminar programme. As issues are raised through the Baseline Studies and the Values-Led Networks we will invite national and international guest speakers and individuals, and groups from across Ireland, to openly debate and develop action strategies. When Céifin is fully operational we will be having at least one of these seminars per month.

In response to change Céifin will undertake research into specific aspects of Irish society in order to drive change based on principles of enduring value. I've spent my life in academia and research but, with respect to all my colleagues, so much of it just ends up on the shelf gathering dust. Céifin research will go beyond studies and reports and feed directly back into the action cycle. As Fr Harry said earlier, we have already commissioned two research studies. The first is into the nature of the family today. What is a family today? What is family life? For all of us our first learning place for human interaction is the family. Do you realise that the last study of family life in Ireland was in 1937?

The economic engine has tended to treat us all as cogs in the machine. But we are more than that. Through our Corporate Network we know that many organisations acknowledge that. We all have responsibilities outside of work. How do the different dimensions of our lives mesh? Dr Miriam Moore's major project is looking at this for Céifin. It will give us an insight into what is needed for balance between work life and family life.

We live in an open world and our problems are not that unique. Others have something to contribute to the debate. Through Céifin we will bring the best of national and international expertise to the table and we'll share the lessons we learn.

On site Céifin will be an exchange forum bringing together a critical mass of top-class researchers in the area of values-led change. Céifin will have a relatively small, dedicated core staff, but that will be backed by a group of researchers on career break or sabbatical. The attachments will be matched to needs and the Institute will be a gateway and focal point for international cooperation.

As new structures replace old, roles change. Céifin intends to play a role in meeting these new professional development needs. We're building relationships with educational partners such as our colleagues here from Dundalk Institute of Technology and the University of Missouri. Together we will take innovative steps to respond to changing roles in the organisation of society.

In our planning of the Institute we have identified four themes and we are working to a five-year plan. Céifin is launched today but Céifin is already a reality.

The Céifin process is a journey from reflection and listening, from question and search, to action and reconnection. From paper to practice, from story-telling to change. It is a challenge for each of us and it is a challenge for every organisation, institution and profession. Our spirits need connection. There is a desperate poverty of spirit abroad. Fulfilment of Céifin's mission will enrich society. We will identify and nurture principles of enduring value that bring balance to people's lives and to foster their embedding in all aspects of life. This is our vision. But, as Peter Senge has said: 'It is not what the vision is, but what it does that matters'.

Together we will create a movement that brings balance and meaning to life.

CÉIFIN
AN INTERNATIONAL PERSPECTIVE

Ron Turner

I come from the University world. Someone defined a university as a circus that never leaves town. But that is the world we come from, and, as you know, there are elephants in the circus, and God knows that there are fleas on some of those elephants. But it is a university world and the university I come from is a public university committed to outreach, research and public service, and the application of knowledge for the benefit of society as a whole. The mission of the twenty-first century university is, in my view, consistent with the mission of the Céifin Institute. I base this view, at least in part, on an important quotation I would like to share with you from the Glion Declaration, which was prepared by ten European University Presidents and ten American University Presidents, who met in Glion, Switzerland, on a mountainside in 1999, to think about what the university should be in the twenty-first century. There is one sentence from that declaration that I believe rings true, for universities and, perhaps, even for Céifin, and it is this: 'In its institutional life, in its professional activities, the university must reaffirm that integrity is the requirement; excellence, the standard; rationality, the means; and very importantly, community, the context; civility, the attitude; and responsibility, the obligation upon which the university's existence and the existence of knowledge itself depend.' Those are high standards and high values and I think that is what this is all about.

I am very pleased to see Céifin's commitment to collective memory, and, specifically, to storytelling, as a means of human expression, as a means of deepening self-awareness and community and family values and a vehicle for creating a larger space for all, for mystery and for creativity. For twenty-two years, I have chaired the St Louis Storytelling Festival on the banks of the Mississippi, where we bring storytellers and story lovers together to tell and hear stories from around the world. Storytelling, I believe, is essential to the agenda for the twenty-first century, as we seek to satisfy what Daniel Yankolovich called 'those sacred expressive yearnings that lie at the heart of the modern search for self-fulfilment'. If there was ever a time that we need to tell stories, if there was ever a time we needed to hear stories from each other, that time is now. Storytelling is a way of caring for ourselves, for our families and for our communities, for our world. And so, when I return to Missouri, to the heartland of America, I will tell the story of this conference, I will tell the story of the Céifin Institute. It is a powerful story – it is a story of hope, it is a story of promise that will resonate with Americans that stand in shock at this time.

In his book, *New Rules; Searching for Self-Fulfilment in a World Turned Up-side-down,* Daniel Yankolovich wrote about community. It is a powerful statement. Let me quote it. He says: 'The idea of community is precious to people, although often they don't know how precious until it is lost. Although difficult to define, abstractly, the idea of community evokes in each individual, here is where I belong. These are my people; I care for them; they care for me. They share my concerns, I know this place, I am on familiar ground, I am at home.' This is a powerful emotion and its absence is experienced through an aching loss, a void, a sense of homelessness; the symptoms of its absence are feelings of isolation and falseness, instability and impoverishment of spirit. I believe the Céifin Institute has the potential to rekindle the concept and the value of community to promote human understanding through caring and concern. It is a worthy goal and sorely needed.

Finally, Fr Harry and Kate, thank you for taking the lead through Céifin, for creating a future which recognises and empowers each individual to grow and to contribute in unique ways to the advancement of life in the twenty-first century. To release human energy, to free the talents and the gifts of each individual, and to nurture the family, build the community and sustain and protect the environment for ourselves and for the future. It is truly a pleasure to be with you, and I hope each of you will join in solid support for this effort and for this institute as we look to the future. In the nineteenth century, an American poet wrote these words at a time of turmoil in our country and I think it is fitting today, and I am reminded of this as I listen to Fr Harry. This poet said: 'Heights by great men and women, were not attained by sudden flight, for they, while their companions slept, were toiling upward in the night'.

INDIVIDUAL RESPONSIBILITY
A Spiritual Perspective

Peter Russell

Let me begin with a brief history of my own journey. I started off as a mathematician and physicist, thinking I was going to be a scientist or a computer engineer. But towards the end of my studies I became increasingly interested in the human mind and human consciousness. I realised that no matter how much physics I studied, I would never answer the fundamental questions about the human mind. Who are we? Why is there consciousness in the cosmos? How does consciousness relate to the brain?

So I took a big step. I left physics and went into experimental psychology, thinking it would answer some of those questions. After finishing a degree in experimental psychology, I knew an awful lot about the brain, about memory, perception and the brain's control of the body. But I don't think the word consciousness had been mentioned once in the whole course.

By this time I had become interested in meditation and Eastern philosophy, and I realised that there were people in the East who had been exploring the mind and consciousness for thousands of years. So I went out to India to study there. That was really the turning point for me. I began to see there was something to religion after all.

As a teenager I had rejected conventional religion. I had been brought up in the Church of England, and at thirteen I went through the process of confirmation. But for me it became a deconfirmation. I realised I simply could not believe things such as the Nicene Creed. If it had to be a choice between what science was telling me and what the Church was telling me, it was clearly science that was going to win for me. I announced to my parents that I wasn't going to church anymore. Fortunately, they said fine. So for the next ten years I considered myself an agnostic – with occasional pangs of atheism.

Two shifts happened when I was in India. First, I saw there was an underlying core to the world's various spiritual traditions. I came to see that spirituality is not so much about spirits or other-worldly phenomena; it is about discovering one's own self, being at peace with one's self in the world, becoming more in touch with a deeper sense of purpose, and freeing the mind from unnecessary fear and anger so that an unconditional love and compassion can emerge.

Second, I realised that many, if not all, of our problems originated from inner human issues. Behind every problem were human decisions, human thinking, human values, and human self-centredness. Everything pointed back to the human being and the human mind. Yet invariably we focused on the problem out there. Whether it was an environmental problem, economic problem, some social problem, or a problem in our personal lives, we looked for solutions in the world around us, rather than within ourselves, where the problem originated. We were tending to the symptoms not the root problem itself.

If you went along to your doctor because of a bad stomach pain, and all the doctor did was give you a pill to take away the pain you would not feel very satisfied. A good doctor would ask what the cause is. Is it something you've eaten? Is it a virus? Or perhaps just stress? But let's find out the cause and treat that as well as the symptoms. Otherwise the problem is likely to keep recurring.

We need to be doing the same with the various problems facing humanity at this critical time. As well as doing all we can to repair the damage we have done to our planet, and to ensure we do no more damage in the future, we also need to ask what is it in ourselves that leads us to behave as we do? If we don't ask those deeper fundamental questions I don't think that we are ever really going to get out of the crisis we are in.

We like to think of ourselves as the most intelligent species on this planet. But it is now becoming clear that we are destroying our planetary habitat. If we carry on as we are, we won't be here in thirty or forty years time. Yet despite this awareness we don't change our behaviour. We continue destroying our habitat. Is this intelligent? It's more like insane. The question we must ask is why? What's wrong with us?

Some people argue that there is an intrinsic fault with humanity. We are self-centred, short-sighted, greedy beings, and that's it. If that were true we may as well pack up and go home now. There's not much hope. But I don't think the problem lies in the way our brains are wired, but in the way we think – in our attitudes, our assumptions, and the programmes that run us – what we think is important in life. In other words, our values.

The Real Bottom Line

When we begin to look at our values we find that there are several layers to them. On the surface we may value things like possessions, money, social status, and the roles we play. But then we need to ask why do we value these things. If you look deeper you find that they are important because they may give us a sense of security, stimulus, acceptance or attention. But why are they things important to us? What's beneath them?

What is it we really want? What is really important to us at a fundamental level?

The answer comes down to something very simple. We want to feel at peace in ourselves; we want to be happy. Basically we are looking to feel OK in ourselves.

This is our true bottom line – how we feel inside. Usually when we talk of the bottom line we mean our material or financial bottom line. But the one thing we all want is to feel happy. We may call it different things – inner peace, fulfillment, contentment – but the truth is we want to feel good inside. I write a book because I get some satisfaction from doing so. I go swimming because I enjoy it. Even things I don't actually enjoy at the time, like going to the dentist, I do because I believe that I'll be happier later in life if I put up with a little discomfort now.

There are two points to notice about this fundamental drive. First, it is common to each and every one of us. As the Dalai Lama once said, 'In the final analysis, the hope of every person is simply peace of mind.' In this respect we are united. Even with the people you don't particularly like, the people you think are stupid, the people you judge as evil, your apparent enemies, and your closest friends, we all want exactly the same.

The diversity amongst us stems not from what we each want at a fundamental level, but the ways we try to find that contentment. Often the way one person tries to find it conflicts with the way another person is looking for it. The conflict lies in the assumptions we have about what will make us happy, but underneath we are all seeking exactly the same thing.

Second, and most importantly, what we are looking for is something internal. We are looking for a better state of mind. It's an internal goal not an external one.

Looking in the Wrong Place

There's nothing wrong with seeking a more satisfying state of mind. Where we have gone wrong is the ways in which we seek it. And that is where our values come in – the assumptions and programming that we bring to bear on events. We've got locked into a belief that says whether or not you are happy and at peace depends upon what you have and what you do. In essence this belief system says that your internal state of mind depends on your external circumstances.

Now that belief does have some validity. If the reason you are not happy is because you are sick, or hungry, or cold, then there may indeed be something in your external environment that needs to be changed. You do need to do something, or get something.

Several hundred years ago, before the Industrial Revolution, the reason most people were not happy was probably to be found in their external circumstances. There was a lot of disease, the winters were hard, and food often in short supply. We today with all our luxuries can easily forget just how hard life could be in former times. We live in a totally different world. Most of us – and by 'us' I mean those here in this room, the more fortunate members of the human race who have the time and money to be able to come to a conference like this – have our basic needs for food, water, shelter and clothing taken care of. If we are still not happy and at peace the chances are that it is something inner that is missing. It could be that we are not feeling recognised, or not loved, or we have a lack of meaning and purpose, or a feeling of insecurity. These are all inner needs. But what has happened is that we are now caught in this belief that says if you're not feeling happy go and do something, go and get something, go and be somebody. Our attention is focused on changing the world 'out there' in order to satisfy some inner need.

This belief is fed to us from the day we are born – by our parents, by education, by the media. I know my parents just assumed this was the right way to bring me up. They were trying to be responsible and ensure I had a good life. I remember when I was about twenty-five, I'd been to visit my parents and was just leaving the house when my mother decided to give me a little talk. She said, 'You've been to university, you've done well and got your degrees, you've travelled round the world, don't you think its about time you got a job?' Being in a more reactionary phase of life, I asked 'Why?' My mother replied that there would come a time when I wanted to get married, buy a house, be able to go on a holiday, and such things. I kept asking 'Why?' and she kept coming up with reasons why it would be good to get a job. Finally, probably out of some frustration, she said 'So that you can be happy, of course.' I said, 'But aren't I happy?' She looked at me and said, 'Well I suppose you are, yes.' And since then, whenever the subject has come up, she's said, 'As long as you're happy, that's the main thing.'

The Root Cause

It is this belief that what we have or do determines our inner happiness that drives consumerism. We believe that buying things can make us happy. I don't think that is the case. It may appear on the surface that things make us happy, but if you look more deeply at what's actually going on, it is clear that we are being told by the advertisers and marketers that we're missing something – the Chanel dress or whatever it is – and that we cannot be happy without it. They create an artificial sense of missing something, and with it an artificial sense of unhappiness. We want something we haven't got, and when we do go and buy it that want goes, and we feel happier again. You feel a wonderful relief, because the wanting has ceased. But it does not last for long. Soon there is something else we believe we need, and again we feel dissatisfied. The point is that it is not the buying of something that makes us happy, but buying it relieves us of the feeling of dissatisfaction that we have created for ourselves.

Much of what we consume we consume not because of some physical need. We consume in order to satisfy some inner need. But since no external thing can ever really satiate an inner need, we keep on seeking, keep on buying, in the vain hope that if only we bought enough of the right things we will eventually find fulfillment. But all along we are looking in the wrong place.

This is brought out in a popular Sufi tale in which the character Nasrudin is out at night on his hands and knees underneath a street lamp in front of his house. His neighbour comes by and asks what he's doing. 'Looking for the key to my house,' says Nasrudin. So the neighbour gets down to help him look for it. After a while, when they still haven't found the key, the neighbour asks where exactly Nasrudin had dropped it. 'Somewhere in my house,' he replies. 'Well why are you looking for it out here?' 'Ah says Nasrudin 'there's more light out here.'

We may laugh, but that in a way is exactly what our society would have us do. We've lost the key to inner fulfillment. But rather than search for the answer inside ourselves we look out to the world around us because there is indeed more light out there. The human mind is still such a mystery. But the external world is a different matter. There's more light there. We know how that works and how to change it. We can reshape it into computers, wonderful clothes, cars, almost anything we can imagine. This is the world we can manage. So we set about controlling it in some way or another, in the hope that we'll create the right circumstances for inner peace.

Advertisers understand this. If you look at any advertisement and analyse it, you'll find that it's basically saying buy this product, this service, this software, this credit card, or whatever, and you will feel better for it. They know what will hook us – but unfortunately they don't tell us that it won't actually work. My favourite example is of a car hire company that used to be just outside Heathrow Airport on the road into London. Outside was a big banner saying: 'Rent from us and be assured peace of mind'. They know that's what we are looking for, but they keep us looking in the wrong direction.

This belief, that if only I had more I would feel better, also lies at the root of so much greed. The more I have, the happier I'll be – or so we think. It likewise underlies the love of money. We love money not for itself. Who would love a little bit of paper or metal, or electronic digits? What we love is the ability of money to buy the things, the experiences, the opportunities, the friends or whatever that we think will bring us peace of mind.

Perhaps the most tragic aspect of this belief is that as well as having damaging effects on the world around us it also damages our inner world. If you live according to the assumption that if only you had or did the right things you'd be fulfilled, then you easily get into an anxious state of mind. You start worrying about how things are going to be in the future. You start thinking: Will I have what I need to be happy? Will people like me? Will I have the security I need? Is my job safe? What's going to happen to the stock market?

The irony is that we are all wanting to be at peace, to feel fulfilled, yet worry produces the very opposite. If you're worrying you're not at peace. Some people seem to spend their whole life worrying whether they're going to be happy in the future. They never stop worrying long enough to be content with the present.

This way of thinking also has a damaging effect on our personal relationships. We begin looking at others and judging them according to how they might help or hinder us in our search for happiness. And when we start judging others we cannot be said to be truly loving them. I'm not talking about romantic love so much as unconditional love – the kind of love that accepts someone as they are, who ever they are. It is not liking them because they are going to be good for you in some way, but honouring the being, however it manifests, whatever we might think of their behaviour.

A Crisis of Consciousness

The crisis facing humanity today is not so much an environmental crisis, a political crisis or an economic crisis; it is essentially a crisis of consciousness – a spiritual crisis. Any crisis, whether it's a domestic crisis, a social crisis, or a global crisis, is a sign that the old way isn't working anymore. This is both a danger and an opportunity. The danger is that if you just continue shoring up the old way of doing things, the crisis doesn't go away. The opportunity inherent in a crisis is to adopt a new way of thinking and acting.

As a species, we've come to a point in time when the old way of thinking doesn't work anymore. The old way says, take from the world, control your surroundings, what you have and what you get is important. This may have worked in the past, but it is not working anymore. It isn't working for our planet – as is clear from the increasing pollution, resource depletion and environmental degradation we see around us. Nor is it working for us human beings. It no longer delivers the satisfaction we seek.

There was an interesting study done back in 1957 in the USA. Researchers polled a cross-section of the American population, asking people if they were happy with their lot in life. Back then, 30 per cent said they were happy with what they had. In 1992, thirty-five years later, they ran the same poll. Now over the intervening years the GNP had more than doubled, the number of square feet that each person had to live in had doubled, the number of cars per family had tripled, the number of television channels had gone up from a handful of black-and-white to hundreds in colour. All those indicators of so-called quality of life had risen. Yet in 1992 the number of people who said they were happy with their lot was exactly the same – 30 per cent. That seems to me to be good evidence that simply raising the material quality of life more and more doesn't actually lead to greater fulfillment.

Inner Freedom

The real challenge today is not how to create even greater freedoms in the world around us, but to start looking inside ourselves, to ask how can we free ourselves? How can we free human consciousness? That is why I am so intrigued by what is happening here with Céifin. It's beginning, in its own way, to address that question.

Until now consciousness is something our culture and science has ignored. We know so much about the material world, from quarks to quasars, from DNA to quantum physics, and we can build wonderful things with this knowledge, but we still don't understand how thoughts arise in the mind. If I look at my own mind I think it would be wonderful if I could switch off 90% of my thinking. Most of it I have to admit is totally useless. Or consider our feelings. It would be nice not to feel so anxious at times, to be more compassionate, but we know very little about how to do that. Nor do we understand much about how to direct the attention. I doubt that any of us can keep our attention on one single thing for a whole minute. Our minds are always wandering.

There are, of course, some who have explored these questions. Mystics, yogis, philosophers and others examined their own minds first hand and looked at how the human mind gets trapped in various habitual patterns. Their quest has been to free the mind, to allow it to be more at peace, and more compassionate. This is probably the most important question that we now need to be asking at this time. How can we free up the human mind?

A Shift in Perception

The answer it appears is much simpler than one might expect. It's an answer that has been discovered time and time again by different people throughout the ages. The Greek philosopher Epictitus put it very succinctly some eighteen hundred years ago: 'People are disturbed not by things but by the view they take of them'. It's not what happens to us that makes us happy or unhappy, its the way we interpret events that is key.

An example that I often use when I'm working in corporations, which gets the point across to people who probably have no interest in anything spiritual, is to ask if being stuck in a traffic jam makes them upset. Most usually say yes. But, despite what seems to be happening, it is not the traffic jam itself that is causing the upset. All a traffic jam can do is stop cars moving. If you're getting stressed, upset, or angry it's because the voice in your head is telling you this isn't good. It's the voice of fear, the voice of worry. You're no longer in the present moment; you're thinking about the future. You're going to be late for that appointment, or late getting home; and if you're late things won't go so well. You may be criticised, or miss something. So you start feeling upset.

Now somebody else could be sitting in the same traffic jam, but be saying to themselves: 'This is wonderful. This is the kind of situation I've been waiting for all day. I'm not having to sit through another boring meeting, nobody is presenting me with their problems, there's no pile of papers to wade through, no computer beeping to tell me I've got an email. I can sit back, put on some music, and relax for five minutes.'

So we have two totally different responses. One person taking a step closer to a heart attack, the other a step closer to enlightenment. The only difference is what is going on inside their head. It has nothing to do with the external world.

The truth is that so much of the suffering and dissatisfaction we experience is self-created. This is what so many of the great spiritual teachers have recognised and taught. It is what the Buddha recognised two-and-a-half thousand years ago. His story is interesting because it closely parallels what is happening in the world today. He was born a prince in a very wealthy family, but in his early twenties he realised that having all these riches didn't bring an end to suffering. So he decided to leave the palace, give up his luxury lifestyle, and set out to seek a way to end suffering. He is said to have spent six years as an ascetic, studying under various yogis and gurus, trying just about everything, including virtually starving himself to death. Then one day he realised that maybe that was all wrong. He was just sitting down under a tree, meditating, when he realised that the causes of suffering lay within and so did the way to end suffering. Some children were passing by and said, 'You're looking very happy today. What's up?' And he replied, 'I am awake'. So the children said, 'We shall call you Buddha', which in the language of the time meant 'the awakened one'.

The Buddha encapsulated his awakening in the four noble truths. The first is that we all suffer. We all experience dissatisfaction in some way or other. The second is the realisation that we create that inner discomfort for ourselves because we desire things to be different than they are. The third truth is seeing that it needn't be this way. As in the example of the traffic jam, there are different ways of seeing anything – some lead to suffering, some don't. The fourth noble truth explores how to change your way of relating to the world so as not to create unnecessary suffering in yourself or others.

We today are in a very parallel situation. We have riches and luxuries far beyond those of Buddha's time. Yet still we find that having almost anything we desire – Chanel dresses, BMWs, or whatever – doesn't bring an end to suffering. And many of us are likewise seeking other ways to end suffering. That is one reason there is such a growing interest in meditation, personal development and alternative spiritual practices. Gradually we are waking up to the same realisation that the Buddha had. We always have a choice about how we see things.

The trick is learning how to make that choice. One thing that I've found very useful is to just ask myself the question: Is there another way of seeing this? Whoever I'm dealing with, whatever I'm faced with, to simply ask if there is another perspective? I don't go looking for something, but turn the question over to my deeper self. When I do that, the still small voice within often comes up with a much more compassionate perspective. One that feels a lot easier, and is freeing for me. And it usually opens up a whole new way of approaching the situation.

Inner Space
The next great frontier for human development is not outer space, but inner space. We have given ourselves wonderful freedoms in the physical world. What we need now is the inner freedom – freedom from out-dated beliefs and values – that will allow us to manage our lives and the world around with wisdom.

To be sure, there's many people in the world that do not yet have as much freedom as we do. Some 85 per cent of the world is still in poverty; 70 per cent of the world doesn't have decent housing; 50 per cent doesn't have even enough food. These are real problems, and they do need attention. But in addition to working to raise the quality of material well-being in others, we also need to be working to raise the inner well-being in our own society.

We don't need yet more material growth. The sort of growth we need is inner growth – the spiritual growth which our culture has turned its back on. To quote Star-Trek, we need to boldly go where no modern culture has gone before – the exploration and development of human consciousness.

We cannot afford not to. If we carry on the way we are going it's pretty clear there is no future for humanity, or rather, a very depressing negative future. We have to begin to move in a new direction.

Not only is this important for dealing with the many challenges that will face us. It is also going to be critical for handling the ever-accelerating pace of life. Whatever the future is going to be like, one thing is certain: the pace of change is going to be going faster and faster and faster. One consequence of this is that it will become increasingly difficult to predict the future. Very few of us could have predicted five years ago where the internet was going to be today; ten years ago, much less so. So how are we going to predict what the future is going to be like in five or ten year's time?

People talk about the winds of change. I think we are going to be in a storm of change, or rather a hurricane of change. In such situations, those individuals and organisations that will thrive will be those that have the greatest flexibility and stability. It's not going to be so much the external things that count, but how we are inside.

For some years I've been arguing that what we need is the equivalent of an Apollo project for the human mind. The Apollo project, you may remember, began when John Kennedy said that if we put sufficient effort and research into the project we could put a man on the moon in ten years. Nine years later the first human beings stood on the moon. The New Apollo Project that I would like to see happen would do the same for human consciousness. It would be saying that it is possible to free the human mind from out-dated assumptions and values. We can step out of our old mindsets. We don't have to continue the way we've been going. There's plenty of examples of people who have done it to know that it is possible. We don't need to remain trapped. What we need is a concentrated research into how to create a shift in values and make inner freedom a practical reality for all people.

To an extent a shift in values is already underway. Over the last thirty years there have been a number of studies on values. These have shown that people are steadily moving away from materialistic values to values that focus on development of the person and greater responsibility for society and the environment. It is happening, but it's not happening nearly fast enough. It needs to be facilitated and encouraged. That is why I personally am so excited by what is happening here and with Céifin.

I also think it is very appropriate that Céifin is being founded in Ireland. Maybe it's one of the few places in the world where it could happen. And maybe this is a chance for Ireland to really lead the world. I say that as a British person, because for the last twelve years I've been spending a lot of time in Ireland. I come here because the values here touch upon the values I knew growing up in England. Sadly, however, as England has succumbed to increasingly materialistic attitudes, these values have waned. And it is happening here too. But Ireland has not yet gone as far down that slippery slope. Here there's a greater chance of still being able to touch the heart. That is still here and while it's here, let's go for it. It may be the best chance humanity has.

> *They cannot scare me with their empty spaces*
> *On stars, beyond stars where no human face is*
> *I have it in me so much nearer home*
> *To scare myself with my own desert places*

Best wishes to Céifin in providing us all with a place to explore our desert places.

Questions and Answers
Q.
Can you give us examples from the Koran, from the writings of Buddha, that speak of the high places, that believers and non-believers are in search of, which is the well of peace and freedom that you spoke about?

A.
I can't give you any particular examples right now. But I do know there are many, and in almost every tradition. The way I look at it is that when we use words like 'high places', we make it something different from us, beyond us. I think what we are about here is our own deeper inner knowing. It's the place within us all that we're not normally in touch with. We are so caught up on the superficial level of the thinking, the feeling of whatever is going on, that we don't usually have access to this

inner knowing. When we do we find out what it is, there is a wisdom, a truth. Charles Handy was talking about this yesterday, the truth of the self. There's a wisdom that is there that we all share. For example, I suspect what I've been saying wasn't really new; some of the examples might have been new, but the basic message was not fundamentally new. Most of what I said I was touching on ideas that we already know deep inside, but it may not get expressed. One thing that spiritual teachings do is to resonate with that deeper wisdom, and allow us to recognise it in ourselves.

Q.

Is there a danger in the kind of spirituality you have presented that it would only search within the self? Is there a danger that by searching only within the self in a narrow way, that we are searching in the wrong place?

A.

I empathise very much with what your saying. What I'm suggesting is that we rebalance our lives, not deny the external or be only involved in the internal. In our culture we've become almost totally focused on the external. What I'm arguing is that we need to create balance. As well as everything that we are doing in the external we need to explore the internal, because that is where we're most stuck.

It's not about going off and becoming a recluse and ignoring the world. I certainly do take times to go away on retreat. It's very nourishing and I come back feeling much more content in myself, and more able to do what I have to do in the world, and a little more compassionate.

Q.

Where would you see the possibilities for ritual collectively and through community with the ideas you're bringing forward?

A.

I think that there is great benefit not for one particular ritual, but for rituals appropriate to your own community and the tradition that you are in. I don't think it is about creating new rituals. It's about bringing meaning, value and significance to whatever rituals you already have. It's the attitude you bring to the ritual that is important So often rituals are just done as formal things, rarely are they thought about or experienced deeply. We often think of a ritual as something you do again and again. A real ritual is something which you engage in, which is a transformative process. So I think it is not about designing new rituals, but enlivening existing ones.

Q.

You said that we've lost the key to our inner world. There are very ancient old traditions and religions saying that until we find again the lost word, life will stay painful and full of suffering. My question is will this lost word come from the scientific world or from the spiritual world? Or do we have to create a new language for a closer and closer meeting between these two worlds?

A.

At the moment the worldviews of science and spirituality are far apart. But I think the key to their rapprochement lies in the nature of consciousness. Science has great difficulty with consciousness. There is nothing in the contemporary scientific worldview that can explain consciousness. It is the one thing none of us can deny, we are all experiencing beings. Yet there is absolutely nothing in physics or any other science that predicts that any living organism should have awareness. That to me says there is something wrong with the current scientific worldview.

What all the old world mysteries and spiritual traditions have said is that consciousness is fundamental to the cosmos.

Science at the moment is trying to explain consciousness in terms of brain activity. But it is not getting very far at all. I think the meeting point will come when science accepts that consciousness is not something to be explained, something that comes out of matter, but consciousness exists as an intrinsic part of everything. When you make that shift you find that nothing in science changes. Maths, physics, chemistry – everything stays exactly the same. But it does open up a whole new understanding of spiritual experience. It allows spiritual experience to be incorporated within a larger scientific worldview without any conflict. So I see the shift that has to happen as accepting consciousness as absolutely fundamental. That's the bridge that will bring the two together.

VIEW FROM THE CHAIR

Doireann Ní Bhriain

It was hard, looking at the agenda for day two of the conference, to see with clarity where it might lead us. A session on consumer rights followed by one on the launch of the Céifin Institute, followed by a spiritual perspective on individual responsibility didn't appear to me at the outset to promise a particular direction. From the previous day, we carried with us ideas about how to manage our lives as individuals and as members of a community, and here we were starting a new day by talking about money, prices, and the right to complain about bad service. But the wisdom of those who programmed the conference was greater than mine, and I for one found myself at the end of the day clearly focused on what was most important.

I don't like being defined as a consumer or that the people around me are defined as such. But like it or not, that is what in a market-driven society we are. And that, according to Carmel Foley, is where we get our power these days. 'Popular democracy is most often practiced in the market place, not the polling booth,' she said. 'The expression of consumer choice through economic choice has become a defining political activity of our times'.

Carmel's exposition of what she called 'the imbalance of power between vendor and buyer' and how the choices we make and the actions we take can redress that balance were a key theme of her interesting and lively presentation. The importance of legislation and of the building of a trusting partnership between consumer and business – to the advantage of both parties – were other themes she touched on. Most importantly, perhaps, she pointed out how few organisations representing the community at ground level made representations to her office on behalf of consumers. She would welcome them with open arms and we should remember that!

The questions and comments from the floor were wide ranging: how to prevent the arrival of junk mail, how to get access to the technology which would allow people to zap out television advertisements and how to prevent overcharging with the euro changeover. We were asked as consumers to insist on using native seeds to propagate indigenous strains of fruit, vegetables and grains rather than the varieties being sold by the multi-national seed companies – this from the Irish Seed Savers Association. We were warned by one speaker of the dangers of what he called 'consumer inertia', while another warned us of the dangers of conflating citizenship with consumerism and referred us to Naomi Klein's *No Logo* to be reminded of how we are targeted and manipulated by market forces.

And finally, we were reminded that looking to the future was all very fine, but that we are in danger of abdicating responsibility for the present. A speaker from the Clare Youth Service asked us to consider, in the context of underage drinking, whether we as adults have been responsible enough in the past. Our young people are entitled to trust us to behave responsibly and to help them to do the same. Mind you, the older generation needs to be careful about laying down the law. One young man who spoke from the floor admonished adults for denying young people the freedom to behave as they wish.

Those who had attended the previous three conferences as well as those of us who were on our first visits were awaiting with great anticipation the launch of the Céifin Institute. Fr Harry Bohan did the honours. He presented an exciting vision for the Institute, spelling out its genesis and its core values. At its heart, it seemed to me, is a desire to examine what really gives meaning to people's lives and to find ways of bringing these values to the surface and making them real in the context of how we live our lives now. The key, said Fr Harry, is listening – 'We'll start out where the people are,' he said. 'Céifin is an investment in people'. He concluded by reading a very welcome letter of support from an Taoiseach, Bertie Ahern.

Kate Ó Dubhchair, Programme Director of the new Institute, presented a more detailed exposé of how Céifin will work and of the research it will undertake. Baseline studies on subjects like planning and diversity, listening to each others' stories, devising models for values-led change, facilitation of mentoring networks, provision of a space where people can take time out to think and reflect, bringing diverse groups together to listen and learn from each other – these were some of the ideas that caught my attention in her stimulating presentation.

The last speaker in this session was Dr Ron Turner, vice-President of the University of Missouri, who talked about his own university and its ethos and about his enthusiasm for the ideas being put forward for the Céifin Institute. Referring to his own university's values, he used words like integrity, excellence, community, civility and responsibility, the latter referring to the obligations on which the university's existence depended. One of the intriguing things about Ron Turner is the fact that he runs a remarkably successful storytelling festival in St Louis every year, which is attended by 20,000 people. He closed his very apposite remarks with a reference to the importance of storytelling as a way of caring for each other and for our communities.

And of course there were questions and not enough time for answers! Among them were the following: How will Céifin make a difference? How will it fit into government mechanisms in a way that ensures its work is taken seriously? Will it tackle citizens' education? Where will it get its funding from? Will it challenge the status quo and raise people's hackles? What is the culture of the Institute? My personal feeling is that these questions and more will need to be answered with clarity over the next while in order to confirm the groundswell of enthusiasm that was clearly evident from the audience at this and previous conferences and to harness that energy into concrete support for the institute.

The closing session of the conference brought us right back to some core questions. Peter Russell in his opening remarks pointed out that all situations of conflict and difficulty are the external manifestations of deeper internal human problems. Until we get the internal balance right, we are only tinkering with the issues by solving the external symptoms. He talked about our society's obsession with wanting more material things and how we continually create unhappiness for ourselves by wanting more. As soon as we satisfy our want, the fulfilment wears off very rapidly and we start wanting again. Our egocentric selves are what is driving society.

It is Peter Russell's contention that we are living through a crisis of consciousness. The challenge we face is one of freeing up the human mind and exploring our inner space. We don't need any more exterior growth but we do need to focus on our inner selves in order to cope with the accelerating rate of change through which we're living – an Apollo project for the human mind was how he described it. In response to some questions, Peter talked of how science has failed to explain consciousness, and how far apart the worlds of science and spirituality are. The question of what spirituality is was raised, with one contributor stating emphatically that he did not have a spirit, but that he was a human being. It struck me that perhaps the word has been overused or misunderstood, particularly by people who have been disillusioned by or who have no interest in formal religion. Perhaps Céifin might look at how language has become devalued, and at how we can retrieve respect for that inner space Peter Russell talks about. I think there are lots of people in Ireland at the moment who have rejected the dogmas, the language and the practice of formal religion but whose inner space is just as active and as needy as that of churchgoers.

That's just an idle thought, one of many I had over the two days of the conference. It was a thought-provoking event in a very real sense. The speakers provoked us into thought, but so too did the audience. I was very conscious of the strength of their ideas, of their commitment to thinking about change and growth and of their willingness to act when called upon. In fact, the presence in that room of so many people who had a genuine engagement with the ideas being discussed and a yearning to be part of whatever change they might lead to was very powerful.

At the close of his session, Peter took us through a short meditation, allowing us to focus our minds before we dispersed into the November darkness. It was the last of those lovely silences we had from time to time, allowing ourselves to inhabit our inner space for a bit, before the external world with all its excitement and its problems invaded that space again.

It was an enriching and an energising experience to have chaired the day. I learnt far more than I gave, and I hope that Céifin will find effective ways of channelling the enthusiasm and idealism that was so evident in the voices of those who spoke on and off the platform.

CONTRIBUTORS

John Hume lives in Derry. He is married to Pat and has three daughters and two sons. Following his involvement in the non-violent Civil Rights Movement and community initiatives in Derry in the late 1960s he was elected to represent the Foyle Constituency in the Stormont Parliament in 1969. He was a founder-member of the SDLP (Social Democratic Labour Party) in 1970 and has been Leader of that party since 1979. He was also elected to the European Parliament in 1979. He was instrumental in negotiating an end to violence leading to the Good Friday Agreement in 1998. He has been the recipient of the Irish People of the Year Awards (1984) the Nobel Peace Prize (1998) and the Martin Luther King Award (1999). He is the first recipient of the Céifin Award (2001).

Charles Handy is a writer and broadcaster whose books have sold well over a million copies around the world. He has been an oil executive, an economist, a professor at the London Business School and the Warden of St George's House in Windsor Castle. He describes himself as a social philosopher, concerned with the changes that technology and capitalism are bringing to our work and lives. His new book is *The Elephant and the Flea* which explores the above topics. His other publications include *The Empty Raincoat* and *The Hungry Spirit*.

Anne Coughlan is a senior researcher with the Irish Business and Employers Confederation (IBEC). She has researched employers' views and practices for almost twenty years on such matters as absenteeism, equal opportunities, education and training needs, accidents in the workplace, competitiveness, reward/payment schemes, and skill shortages. More recently she completed a major study in the area of flexible working arrangements in the high-tech manufacturing sector.

Freda Donoghue is Senior Research Fellow at the Centre for Non-profit Management in the School of Business Studies, Trinity College. She holds a PhD in Sociology from the University of Leicester (1991) for her thesis on agency temporary workers and is the co-author of *Women and Political Participation in Northern Ireland* (with Rick Wilford and Robert Miller; Avebury, 1996). Dr Donoghue has published several pieces of note on the voluntary sector in Ireland and is a founding member and now Chair of the Association for Voluntary Action Research in Ireland. She is also a member of the National Committee on Volunteering.

Tom Healy is currently working with the Department of Education and Science following a leave of absence for five years to work with the Organisation for Economic Co-operation and Development in Paris. His work at OECD focused on the role of education and lifelong learning in promoting well-being and economic growth. He was principal author of *Human Capital Investment – an international comparison* (1998) *and The Well-Being of Nations – the role of human and social capital* (2001), both published by OECD.

John Quinn has been a senior producer with RTÉ Radio 1 since 1977. His programmes have won numerous distinctions, including three Jacobs Awards, and international awards in Japan and New York. His weekly educational magazine programme *The Open Mind* is now in its thirteenth year. He has written five novels, four for children, and has edited three best selling publications from his radio programmes: *Portrait of An Artist as a Young Girl, My Education* and *The Open Mind Guest Lectures 1989-1999*.

Carmel Foley is a native of Athlone. She has been Director of Consumer of Affairs since 1998. Her current appointments include the North-South Food Safety Promotion Board, the Euro Changeover Board of Ireland and the Liquor Licensing Commission. She is former Chief Executive of the Employment Equality Agency and Council for the Status of Women. From 1978 to 1989 she worked with the Department of Foreign Affairs diplomatic service including postings to Washington and Luxembourg.

Fr Harry Bohan is a native of Feakle, County Clare. Following his ordination, he studied Sociology in the University of South Wales, Cardiff, where he received an MSc. Econ. He is recognised as one of the leading social commentators in Ireland during the past twenty five years and has been the driving force behind several practical projects aimed at strengthening family and community, including the Rural Housing Programme. He instigated the 'Our Society in the New Millennium' series of national conferences which have been held annually since 1998.

Kate Ó Dubhchair is a native of Derry. Formerly a Senior Lecturer with the University of Ulster she joined the Project Development team for the Céifin Institute in 1999. Concurrently she is Professor of Community Informatics in the Truman School of Public Affairs, University of Missouri. She holds an MSc in Computing. A social scientist, her doctoral thesis brought together computing and sociology and focused on the development of the parameters of a knowledge infrastructure for a learning community in the Information Society.

Ron Turner is Executive Vice President and Director of Cooperative Extension for the University of Missouri System. Dr Turner holds the distinction of being the first American to receive an honorary doctorate from a historically black South African university. He serves as a Trustee of the Céifin Institute and oversees the UM System's link with the University of Ulster, National University of Ireland-Galway, and Teagasc. He is founder and honorary chairman of the St Louis Storytelling Festival.

Peter Russell studied physics and experimental psychology at the University of Cambridge, and has a postgraduate degree in computer science. He was one of the first to present personal development programs to business. Over the past twenty years, he has been a consultant to IBM, Apple, American Express, Barclays Bank, Swedish Telecom, Nike, Shell, British Petroleum and other major corporations. His books include *The Brain Book, The Global Brain Awakens, The Consciousness Revolution, Waking Up in Time* and *From Science to God.* He also created the award-winning videos *The Global Brain* and *The White Hole in Time.*

Doireann Ní Bhriain is a broadcaster, arts consultant, wife, mother and lover of the arts and the open air. She worked for over twenty years as a presenter and producer on RTÉ television and radio. From 1993 to 1996 she was Irish Commissioner of *l'Imaginaire Irlandais,* a festival of contemporary Irish culture which took place in France. She returned to RTÉ for a year to organise the 1997 Celtic Film and Television Festival, and left again in 1998 to become general manager of Millennium Festivals.